GOOD HOUSEKEEPING
Cooking with Herbs and Spices

GOOD HOUSEKEEPING
Cooking with

Compiled by
GOOD HOUSEKEEPING INSTITUTE

and produced in collaboration with
SCHWARTZ SPICES

EBURY PRESS *London*

Herbs and Spices

Drawings by JULIA KILLINGBACK
Colour photographs by BARRY BULLOUGH

First published in Great Britain 1975
by Ebury Press,
Chestergate House, Vauxhall Bridge Road,
London SW1V 1HF

First impression 1975
Second impression 1976
Third impression 1977

ISBN 0 85223 073 7

Edited by Gill Edden

Filmset and printed in Great Britain by
BAS Printers Limited, Wallop, Hampshire
and bound by
Webb Son & Co. Ltd.
London and Glamorgan

Contents

Recipes marked with a ✳ are specially
recommended for slimmers

Colour Plates

Foreword

For centuries herbs and spices have been used to enhance the flavour of food. The art of choosing the right herb or spice has always been second nature to cooks who love to serve the natural foods of their country in the most appetising way. In a convenience food age this skill is in danger of dying but it's needed all the more to bring taste and individuality to the mass produced foods we buy today.

The Good Housekeeping Institute team of experts have devised, cooked and tasted all the recipes in this book. They have used a great variety of herbs and spices and the results show what a difference these can make to otherwise ordinary dishes.

Try these that we've made for you and then try out your own ideas. The home economist cookery team responsible were Margaret Coombes, Valerie Barrett, Jill Hughes and Zoe France.

Cassandra Kent researched and wrote the text.

If you have any queries about the recipes in this book write to us at Good Housekeeping Institute, Chestergate House, Vauxhall Bridge Road, London SW1V 1HF.

CAROL MACARTNEY
Director

Introduction

Herbs, spices and their various uses have been known to man since time immemorial. They have played an integral part in cooking the world over and were also an important trading factor from biblical times onwards. This has meant that the culinary use of herbs and spices in different countries has not been restricted simply to those which are native to them.

Today, fortunately, we don't have to await the arrival of ships from far-flung places to keep our larder shelves stocked with herbs and spices. Technological development has meant improved drying methods and the right packaging for maximum storage life, so that we can now buy a wide variety in virtually every supermarket and grocer's shop. This huge distribution means that manufacturers can, to some extent, absorb cost fluctuations caused by good and bad crops from year to year. The major herb and spice houses have generations of experience behind them and know where in the world to go in order to obtain the best quality raw materials.

What is a herb?

The horticultural definition of a herb is any plant whose stem dies down completely in winter. It may revive again the following year or need to be replanted according to its type. There are many hundreds of herbs, but this book is concerned solely with the most commonly used culinary varieties.

Herbs grow generally in temperate climates and can usually be distinguished from spices by the fact that they can be used fresh and are generally less pungent and more delicate in flavour. It is not always easy to isolate where a herb ends and a spice begins though since some plants, for example dill and fennel, have leaves which can be classified as herbs and seeds which are spices. In the glossaries that follow these are indicated by cross-reference.

What is a spice?

Spices are the dried parts of aromatic plants, usually the fruit or seed, though sometimes the bark, root or flower bud. They come, on the whole, from hot countries and add more zest and seasoning to foods than herbs. The early use of spices in cooking was in many instances to mask the taste of meat or fish that was going off.

Historical usage

The earliest known record of herbs and spices actually being eaten comes from Egypt, about 2000 B.C., and it is known that onions and garlic were fed to the men building the Pyramids to safeguard their health. The Egyptians also used them in religious rites and in embalming and medicine. The Bible contains many references to herbs and spices and their great cost, showing how highly they were valued, and the Greeks and Romans used them extensively for cooking, medical purposes, cosmetics and religious rites.

It was in fact the Romans who spread the word to Britain, bringing 400 hitherto unknown varieties with them when they occupied the country. In addition to their culinary and medical uses they became the focus of much superstition and some beliefs still linger today in remote country districts. During the Saxon and Danish period in Britain interest in herbs and spices waned, but it revived considerably with the spread of Christianity during the sixth century as a growing number of monks built monasteries with extensive and carefully tended gardens. Herbs were at this time used in Christian church ceremonies.

In the eleventh, twelfth and thirteenth centuries the Crusaders discovered in the East spices as yet unknown, and brought them back to Europe and Britain. Further varieties became known when, in the fifteenth and sixteenth centuries, explorers discovered America and the West Indies. By the sixteenth century the spice trade had become highly competitive and various nations raced the sea and overland spice routes to establish control over the bulk and the best of the crops. Come the nineteenth century, the sea power of the British navy made London the centre of the world's spice trade.

Herbs also reached their peak use around the sixteenth century. They by then had numerous household uses and were grown in gardens from cottages to manor houses. The Elizabethan herb garden was an intricate design with each herb growing separately, often hedged into little beds by a low-growing line of lavender, rosemary or box. A well-stocked garden would probably have over fifty kinds, some of which would be used for cooking, some for medical purposes, others for strewing on the floor or carrying in posies known as tussie-mussies to keep germs at bay and ward off the smell of the unwashed masses.

Some herbal remedies are still used today and we can even now read the weighty tomes of Culpeper and Gerard (whose *Herball* weighed 5 kg at first printing) and learn what herbs were thought to cure which ills. Reading may produce the feeling that there is no need ever to visit a doctor if you have a herb garden but it is, in fact, not sensible to follow the dictums of the old herbalists blindly since history does not reveal whether they cured more people than they killed and science has subsequently shown that many of the herbs formerly used medicinally are poisonous. Nevertheless, even with the development of synthetic drugs, there are still certain ones which are obtained from natural sources and interest in homeopathic treatment is higher today than it has been for the past hundred years.

The herb cult declined during the nineteenth century and only the basic mint, parsley, sage and thyme figure in recipes of that period. Now, however, there is a considerable revival of interest in herbs and spices for cooking which has, in its turn, led to an increase in the varieties we can buy. This renewed interest is partly a result of increased leisure which has encouraged many people to experiment with different recipes, partly because in a technological age many people find reassurance in using natural products and partly because much of today's food has been processed to a degree of blandness intended to appeal to the maximum number of people and this can be adjusted to suit personal tastes by the addition of herb or spice flavouring.

For those who would like to know more about the background history of herbs and spices, their accompanying lore and their uses through the ages, there are many good books published. This one is intended to help you cook with the most widely available culinary varieties. In the following pages we give hints on using, storing and cultivating (where possible) herbs and spices. The glossaries indicate some additional dishes for further experiments in this kind of cooking.

Cook's Know-how

Flavouring with herbs and spices is an area where the cook can experiment and can increase or lessen the quantity used with little effort and often good effect. Those unaccustomed to seasoning their food in this way should start with only small quantities and build them up to suit their own taste. It is important to remember that herbs and spices are today used to improve and enhance the flavour of foods, not to obscure the taste of what they are added to, as it was in the days when they covered up for the lack of refrigeration. The only cases where this does not apply are with strong spices such as curry powder or ginger, where the dish is based on the overall flavour of the spice.

Dried herbs have a much stronger flavour than fresh and quantities should be adjusted accordingly when following a recipe. In this book we have taken the equivalent measures as 15 ml (one level tablespoonful) of dried to 45 ml (three level tablespoonfuls) of fresh chopped herbs. Using the recipes should give some idea of the quantities of herbs and spices you will need to add when experimenting with other dishes. When you are making up a recipe yourself it is sensible to start off with just a little herb or spice and increase the amount gradually. Be careful not to add too many flavours at a time. Most dishes will taste better if you pick just one or perhaps two to bring out the flavour of the basic ingredients.

When to add herbs

Herbs should ideally be added at different times to different dishes, though in practice they are usually added at the beginning of preparation. In soups and stews they should be put in during the last hour of cooking and it is a good idea to put them in a small cheese cloth or muslin bag and remove them before serving, after their flavour has permeated the dish. Add them to vegetables, sauces and gravies for the last ten minutes cooking. In meat loaves, pâtés, stuffings and beefburgers add them when mixing the other ingredients, at the beginning. With roasts and grills they should be sprinkled on during cooking. In uncooked mixtures like salad dressings, dips and juices the herbs should be added several hours before serving to allow the flavour to develop. Never allow subtle herbs to be overpowered by other ingredients; for instance it's often better to use lemon juice rather than vinegar in salad dressings to allow the herb flavour to come through.

When to add spices

Ground spices give up their flavour more quickly than whole ones and should be added to a stew towards the end of a long or medium cooking time. Whole spices can be put in at the beginning, suspended in a muslin bag if you want to remove them before serving. For curries and cold dishes all spices should be added when you are preparing the ingredients. For grills and roasts spices should be rubbed into the surface of the meat before cooking. In cakes and pies add them when mixing the dry ingredients; it is a good idea to combine them with the sugar before blending with the other ingredients as this ensures more even distribution. With uncooked dishes spices should be added well in advance of serving and given time to release their flavours.

All spices will be more aromatic if they are placed on a baking sheet and heated at about 160°C (300°F) mark 2 for 5–10 minutes.

What goes with what?

There are very few rules about which herb or spice goes with which food, though certain classic uses have evolved. Even so, these are not hard and fast rules and part of the pleasure of cooking with these seasonings is for the cook to add her own touches. In the glossaries we suggest some dishes for experiment beyond the recipes in this book and it is also well worth trying the addition of some seasonings to ready processed or frozen foods to give a touch that lifts them out of the ordinary.

Flavours in the freezer

Herbs and particularly strong spices continue to develop their flavours while in a freezer so it is important to remember this when seasoning a dish that you are going to store for some time. Up to about two months in a freezer will not make much difference to the original flavour of the herb or spice but after that it will begin to change and over a period of, say, nine months will compare unfavourably with the way it tasted when freshly cooked. Where possible it is therefore advisable to add herbs and spices after thawing and before or during reheating. With foods such as cakes or biscuits where this is not possible, the freezer storage period should be kept to less than two months.

Good for health

Most herbs and spices contain a number of nutritional elements such as vitamins, alkaloids, essential oils and minerals as well as the more basic proteins, starches and sugars. While you are obviously not going to improve your nutritional intake all that much with just a pinch here and a pinch there, it is worth remembering that these and other properties of the herbs lead to advantages such as stimulation of the appetite, assistance with digestion and relaxation. For people on special diets, particularly those that rule out salt, the milder herbs and spices can be used to give interest and variety to food. Some are also beneficial to people with ulcers and other stomach troubles while slimmers and sufferers from diabetes will find angelica and sweet cicely useful sugar substitutes when cooking tart fruits.

Herbal teas

Herbal teas have always been popular in continental Europe though in Britain until recently they could usually only be found as musty sachets hidden at the back of health food shops. Today, however, there is a revival of interest in herb teas. They lack the stimulating tannin and caffeine of the hot tea and coffee that most people drink most of the time and so can be used to soothe and relax, aiding indigestion or insomnia.

You can buy herbal teas ready prepared in sachets or make your own, either from bought dried herbs or from your own fresh or dried varieties. With fresh herbs you need about 15 ml (one level tablespoonful) for one cup of tea, with dried herbs about 5 ml (one level teaspoonful).

To dry your own herbs for teas, or tisanes as they are often called, use the same methods as when drying for cooking (see page 17), remembering that there is no need to break down the leaves into such small particles since they will be strained when the tea is poured. Herbs that make good tisanes are angelica, balm, bergamot, caraway, chamomile, comfrey, dandelion, fennel, hyssop, marjoram, peppermint and spearmint, purslane and sage.

Outside the kitchen

The non-culinary uses of herbs are legion. Books are published on making your own herbal remedies and herbal cosmetics and there are also many variants of scented and attractive mixtures which can be placed in bowls as *pot pourri* to scent a room, or used as a filling for sachets and small pillows and used in drawers and linen cupboards.

One of the most popular and easy ways to scent a cupboard is with a pomander. These were originally mixtures of aromatic herbs and spices carried in a round perforated container to ward off infection and smells. Today the base is usually made of an orange which should be studded closely with cloves until there is no skin showing. The orange should then be rolled in a mixture of equal parts of ground cinnamon and powdered orris root to give added perfume and 'fix' the scent so that it does not deteriorate. Then leave it in a cool, dry place for about five to six weeks until it has completely dried through and probably shrunk slightly so that there is no space between the clove heads. The pomander is now completed and may be placed in a drawer or tied round with ribbon and hung in a cupboard. Powdered orris root is available from Culpeper House Ltd., 21 Bruton Street, London W1. Check the price before ordering.

Pot pourri can be made by anyone who has a flower garden or access to a variety of flower petals. The best base is rose petals and to these you can add scented flowers or leaves such as lavender, rosemary, carnation, orange blossom, acacia, jasmine, lemon verbena, bay or balm. Some bright blue borage flowers will make the mixture look attractive and thinly peeled orange or lemon rind will add to the aroma.

The flower petals should be dried in a warm, airy place. Then place the rose petals in a jar with a well fitting lid and mix a small handful of common salt with each large handful of rose petals. These should be left for five days and stirred twice daily. At the end of this time the rose petals, salt and other dried flowers and leaves should be combined. Add to them a mixture of

125g (4 oz) powdered orris root	2–3 cinnamon sticks
25g (1 oz) coriander seed	15 ml ($\frac{1}{2}$ oz) oil of geranium, optional
25g (1 oz) grated nutmeg	15 ml ($\frac{1}{2}$ oz) oil of lavender, optional
25g (1 oz) whole cloves	

The oils can be obtained from good chemists, including Savory & Moore Ltd., 143 New Bond Street, London W1 (check prices at time of order) but are fairly expensive and may be omitted. As alternatives you can add some allspice or mace to give more aroma.

If oils are used they should first be mixed with the orris root then combined with the other spices. Otherwise add all the spices to the flower petal mixture, stirring well. Cover this and leave for three to four weeks, stirring from time to time. If it is too moist, add more orris root; if too dry, add extra salt or more flower petals. At the end of this time the *pot pourri* is ready for use in bowls or sachets.

Storing Herbs and Spices

Storage is all-important if your herbs and spices are to stay in peak condition for as long as possible. Fresh herbs are not too much of a problem. If you grow them yourself they should be picked literally the moment you intend to throw them into the pot. Bought fresh herbs should be purchased as near as possible to the time when you intend to use them, though the tougher ones like mint, parsley and chives will keep for a few days in a tumbler of water or in the fridge salad crisper.

Shop bought dried herbs come in a variety of containers. If they are in a sealed packet, leave them as they are until you need to open the packet; then transfer the remaining herbs to an airtight jar. Glass is the best container for dried herbs and tinted glass gives the added advantage that they can then be left on open shelves as the light will not penetrate so easily. Paper bags tend to absorb the oils in the herbs and spices and plastic containers can produce 'sweating' if they are not kept scrupulously clean and moisture-free. The lids

should be airtight. Keep your herbs out of daylight and away from direct heat –
a larder or cupboard is a suitable place. Both light and heat will destroy their
aromatic qualities fairly quickly. The bunches of dried herbs found hanging
from some kitchen ceilings look pretty but probably will not be much good for
flavouring after a few weeks.

Buy herbs and spices in small quantities only, as their life is so short. If your
storage arrangements are good, it is worth buying up to a year's supply but
no more. It is useful to know when each variety is likely to reach the shops with
the new year's crop. Buying then means you get it in peak condition; buying at
intervals during the same year you will obviously be getting the same vintage –
its quality will depend on the shop's storage facilities.

Bulk bought herbs should be stored in the dark somewhere cool while you
decant small quantities into the little jars that are going to stand near your
cooker. This way the bulk supply should retain its freshness longer. Spice
houses go to a lot of trouble to trap as many of the volatile oils as possible when
harvesting and packing and it is a pity to let their efforts go in vain because of
lack of care in the home.

Keep herb and spice jars tightly sealed at all times. Open them the minute you
want to use them and close them again as soon as you have taken out the right
quantity. Take a sniff at them from time to time; if there is no aroma at all you
may as well throw them out and buy new ones. It's false economy to keep them
too long or to insist on using up the very last of a jar if all the savour has gone
from it.

Drying herbs at home

Home-grown or bulk bought fresh herbs can be preserved in a number of
ways. The traditional method is drying and most of our ancestors were expert
in the stillroom techniques needed to ensure sufficient supplies of each herb
and spice for culinary, medicinal and cosmetic purposes. To dry herbs successfully you should pick them when the dew is just off, before the sun gets to them
and disperses the volatile oils. The best time is just before they are due to flower,
when they contain the maximum amount of these valuable oils. After picking,
go through the herbs, handling them very carefully to avoid bruising. Throw
out any that are damaged or yellowed or past their best. Dusty stems and leaves
may be rinsed quickly in cold water; otherwise, to avoid excessive handling, it
is probably best to hope that the dew has cleaned them for you.

Herbs can be dried in the sun over a period of four to five days. This method
does tend to make them lose their green colour and some of their aromatic
properties though. It is quicker and better to dry them in an airing cupboard or

the oven, both with the door left slightly ajar to allow air to circulate. The oven temperature should not exceed 32°C (90°F). Place the herbs on wire racks covered with muslin or cheesecloth which lets the air through and from time to time turn the herbs gently to ensure quicker, more even drying.

You can tell when they are dry because the stem and leaves will become brittle but still green and will crumble easily when rubbed between the fingers. If you are not quite sure about this, check by putting the dried herbs into a glass jar, cover it and watch for a few days to see if moisture appears. If it does, turn them out and continue the drying process. If the leaves turn brown you know that they have been overdried and are of no further use.

It is also possible to dry herbs in hanging bunches in a dry place. Pick the stems as long as possible, tie them loosely in small bunches and suspend them out of direct sunlight. If this is difficult place them in brown paper bags and hang them up. Check at regular intervals after three days until they are fully dry. Once dried you can strip the leaves from the stems and crumble them for storage. Don't rub so hard that they turn to dust or, again, some of the flavouring properties will be lost.

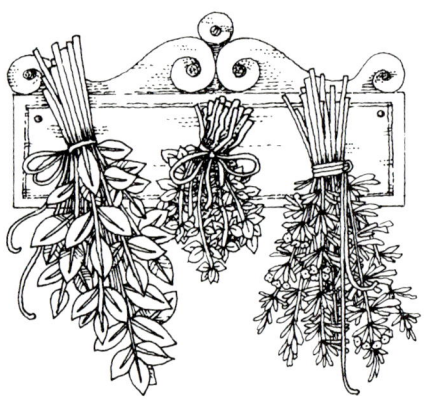

Freezing herbs

Some herbs, for example chives, dill and fennel, do not dry well and are best frozen if you own a freezer. Others such as parsley, basil and tarragon have very tender leaves and also lend themselves well to freezing. They don't take up much space and, if frozen in one-dish quantities, can be taken straight from the freezer for sprinkling on a finished dish or adding to the cooking. If you are not going to store them for more than about two months they can be frozen straight after picking. If you want them to have good keeping qualities it is as well to blanch them for just under a minute before freezing. Tie them in bunches with a long string and just dip them into boiling water, then chill in cold water. Pack in freezer bags or foil or make into frozen herb cubes by chopping up a small quantity into each section of an ice cube tray and topping up with stock. Once frozen these can either be stored in the trays, covered with foil, or removed and stored in polythene bags.

Herb vinegars

Herbs and their flavours will be preserved automatically if you use them in pickles, chutneys or dishes for your freezer. Another good way of using them is in herb vinegars which can be used to give the appropriate herb flavour to any dish that requires vinegar. Practically all herbs can be used in a vinegar: good ones are tarragon (marvellous in French dressing), thyme, sage and rosemary. All are excellent in marinades for meat.

To make a herb vinegar you take about 90 ml (6 tablespoonfuls) of chopped fresh herbs to 600 ml (1 pint) of vinegar. Warm the vinegar – wine vinegar is best though others will do – and pour it on to the herbs. Cover the jar with

waxed paper and screw on a lid. Leave it for about two weeks, shaking the bottle every day, then taste it to see if the flavour is sufficiently pronounced. When it is, strain the vinegar into bottles and push a fresh stem of the herb into the bottle. This will not add flavour but looks attractive and serves as a reminder if the label comes off.

Herb salts and sugars

Herb salts are very handy for spicing up convenience foods and soups. They will improve all packet mixes, though you should check first whether these have been pre-salted. They can also be used when you are cooking vegetables, instead of plain salt. To make a herb salt mix equal quantities of the chosen herbs and non-iodized salt. Spread it on a baking sheet and put it in a very low oven with the door left slightly ajar for about half an hour. The warmth releases essential oils from the herbs and these are then absorbed by the salt. When the salt is thoroughly cool store it in a screw-top jar.

Herb sugars do not need heat. You make them like vanilla sugar; just put a sprig of the fresh herb in a jar of caster sugar, seal it and leave the herb to scent and flavour the sugar over a period of time. When you come to use the sugar you can either remove the leaves or add them to the dish along with the sugar. Herb sugars are delicious in custards and sweet soufflés, or sprinkled on to cakes, biscuits and sweet pastries. Two herbs that give an unusual flavour to sugar are peppermint and lemon balm. Both are excellent used on fruit salads.

Grinding your own spices

Spices should be given the same care as herbs. People who grind their own, buying them whole, will find that they last longer and give off a better flavour than those bought ready ground. Spices can be ground in various ways. If you are doing a large quantity, an electric or hand coffee grinder does the job quickly and efficiently but you must take care that it is thoroughly cleaned beforehand and afterwards so that no cross-flavouring occurs. An effective way to do this is to wipe the grinder out with kitchen paper then pulverise one or two slices of stale bread to take up the smell. Alternatively you can put the spices through a pepper mill but this takes a long time, even just to get a couple

of tablespoonfuls, and also scents the mill. You might think it worth keeping a special mill for, say, coriander if you grind this particular spice a great deal. The easiest method of all is simply to crush the spices on a board with a rolling pin or in a pestle and mortar.

Drying spices

Most people do not grow their own spices as they are so readily available in shops and of such good quality. Usually it is not worth the trouble of cultivating a few plants for the small seed yield you will get. But if you are growing plants such as dill, fennel and anise for their leaves you may think it is worth allowing them to flower and go to seed as well. If so, these can be dried in the home in the same way as herbs, left in their pods where they have them. Once dry the pods should be rubbed off gently and the seeds put in clean, dry jars. Watch out that no insects get in with them!

Herbs

Angelica (*angelica archangelica*)
Usually the stems only are used, candied and crystallised, to decorate cakes and pastries and as a flavouring in jam. In fact the whole plant can be used – the leaves as a flavouring for fish and the root for stewing with tart fruit such as rhubarb, in place of sugar. The stems can also be eaten like celery. Angelica grows easily as a biennial and may reach heights of 2 m (10 ft) so should be kept to the back of the herb garden or used as a windshield for other plants. It likes shady places and has large pale green leaves with marked indentations and thickish stems. It usually flowers only in the second year but dies after that. Legend has it that the name of the plant comes from the angel who revealed its curative properties for the plague. It was also used in the seventeenth century as a cure for the bites of mad dogs. Angelica makes a good herbal tea (both stem and leaves are used).

Almond tutti-frutti cake *page 142*

Anise (*pimpinella anisum*)
This is grown and sold mainly for its seed form (see page 40). The leaves may be used to flavour soups and stews or to give an unusual touch to fruit salads. It grows best in sunny areas such as India, North Africa, Spain and Italy but can be cultivated in Britain in sheltered places, although the fruits will only ripen when the summer has been really hot. It has light green serrated leaves and white flowers. It is possible to harvest the seeds for use in cooking but you are unlikely to obtain large quantities.

Balm (*melissa officinalis*)
Balm was originally a Middle Eastern plant but is now grown in most Mediterranean countries and will also flourish in Britain. It has a lemon scent and flavour and has been known since the Romans brought it to Britain as a herb that cheers people up and makes them merry. It goes well in fish and poultry dishes, sauces and marinades and as a lemony addition to sweet dishes and hams. Balm makes a good tisane that is said to promote relaxation. Bees love balm and many bee keepers rub the insides of their hives with it to keep the bees at home. It grows easily in most soils but has a creeping root system that should be kept under control or it will take over the whole herb garden. Balm, like

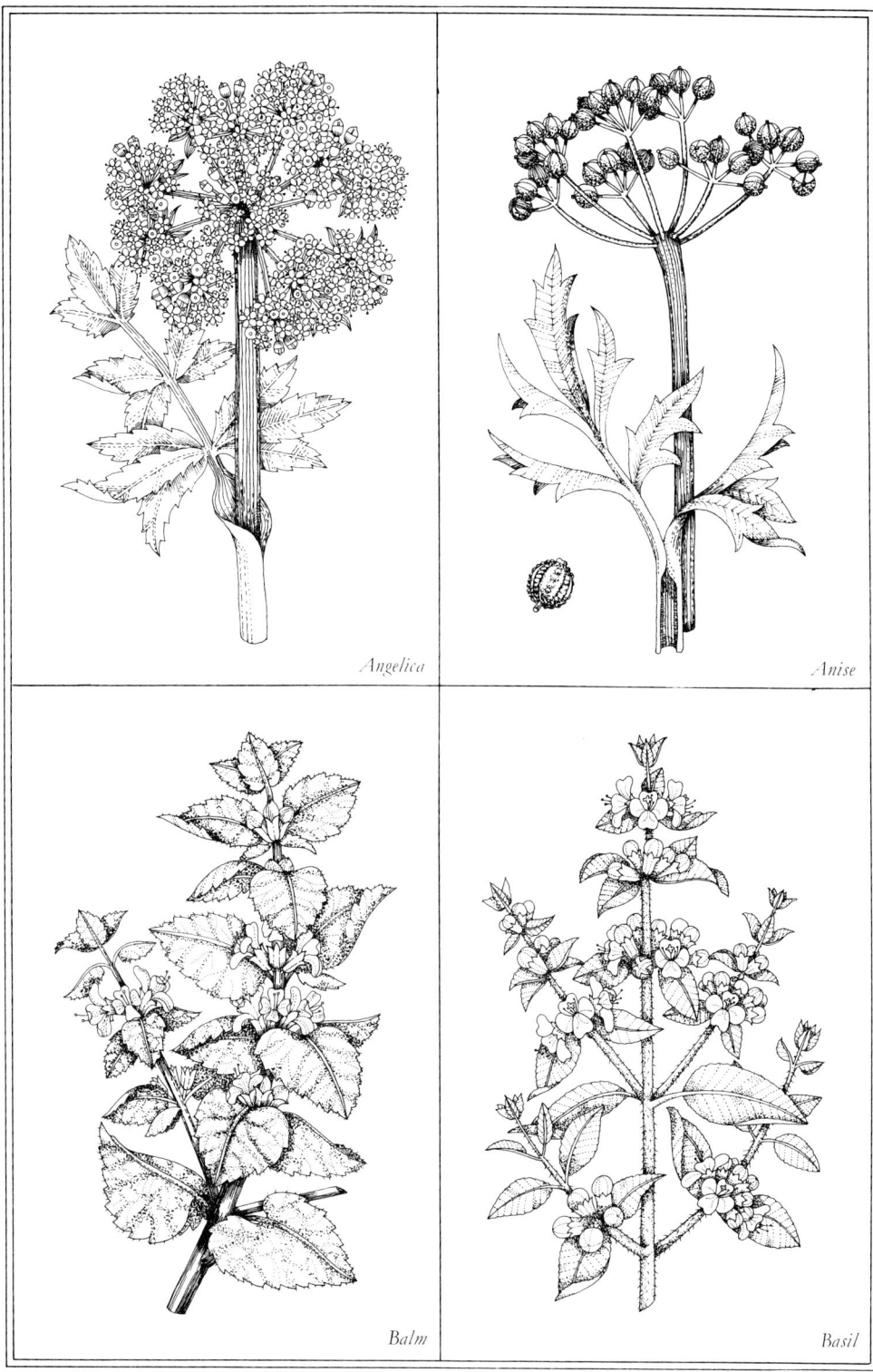

Angelica

Anise

Balm

Basil

mint, should be grown in a bottomless tin bucket sunk into the earth or in a small bed on its own. It has pale green heart-shaped leaves and attractive creamy flowers that will bloom for most of the summer, adding some colour to the herb garden. For use in cooking it should not be allowed to flower, but the buds should be pinched off to encourage further leaf growth.

Sweet yoghurt dressing *page 153*

Basil (*ocimum basilicum*)

Also called Sweet Basil to distinguish it from bush basil, which is an ornamental plant. The leaves can be used fresh or dried in salads, stuffings and poultry dishes. They give spectacular improvement to tomatoes and are used a great deal in Italian cookery. To grow basil pick a sunny spot and nip off the flowers as they appear, in order to lengthen the flourishing period. Basil is a fairly low growing plant with bright but pale green leaves that are spade-shaped. The small flowers, if allowed to appear, are white and grow in the angles of the leaves. Basil can be grown successfully indoors during summer months but tends to shoot up and become spindly unless pinched out at regular intervals.

Avocado with herb dressing *page 66*
Cheese baked tomatoes with basil *page 66*
Cheese baked eggs *page 74*
Crisp top casseroled beef *page 77*
Pork with herbs in cider *page 79*
Tangy chops *page 81*

Cod cutlets in mushroom cream sauce *page 87*
Spaghetti bolognese *page 100*
Whole bean provençale *page 111*
Tossed fresh spinach salad *page 123*
Salade niçoise *page 126*

Bay (*laurus nobilis*)

In ancient times this was believed to be a magic plant that gave protection against the devil. The Romans wore it as a wreath to indicate success or victory and it was used in Britain in the Middle Ages as a strewing herb, for its scent and antiseptic properties. Bay has a strong spicy flavour which becomes stronger with drying. It is an essential ingredient of *bouquet garni* and also goes well in fish dishes and in soups and stocks. You can buy powdered bay, which is fairly strong but sometimes less trouble to use than the whole leaf. A bay tree or bush is an attractive addition to most gardens and it also grows very successfully in tubs. You can prune it like a hedge to get a shape that you like. The long pointed leaves are dark green and shiny on top, paler and veined underneath. The greenish flowers are followed by purple berries but neither show up well against the dark branches and leaves. Although it is said that the wicked flourish like the green bay tree, it should be kept out of frosts (put sacking round the base) especially while small and young. Bay trees can grow very tall although pruning should keep them to a manageable height.

Bay

Borage

Bergamot (*monarda didyma*)

Like balm, this is a bee-attracting plant used mainly in herbal teas. The leaves and flowers make an unusual addition to salads and pork dishes. Bergamot is not sold commercially so you must grow it yourself to obtain the fresh leaves. It is a perennial plant so once started will grow for many years; it has roughish, slightly hairy leaves and red flowers, both of which can be used when making a tisane.

Borage (*borago officinalis*)

Borage leaves have a slightly salt, cucumber-type flavour and the bright blue flowers are also edible. They add a refreshing attractive touch to cold punches and Pimms and can be used fresh or candied. The fresh leaves go well in salads, especially with cucumber where they set off the flavour. The flowers may be floated on fruit salads. Borage had a great reputation as a cheering herb in the sixteenth century and the herbalist Gerard claimed that 'Borage gives courage'. It grows well in Britain and is attractive to bees. It is a medium-high plant (up to 1 m, 2–3 ft) that flourishes even in poor soil. It has large, greyish leaves that are slightly hairy and once sown will continue to reseed itself.

Bouquet garni

This is a small bunch of herbs tied together and suspended by string into meat, game and poultry dishes. The classic *bouquet garni* consists of bayleaves, parsley stalks and sprigs of thyme. For other dishes appropriate herbs may be added, or substitutes. If you are making a *bouquet garni* from dried herbs they should be tied in a small muslin bag and removed before the dish is served. It is possible to buy ready made up sachets of *bouquet garni* which are quick and easy to drop into dishes for cooking. These should be used up fairly quickly as they will otherwise lose some flavour and aroma. They should always be stored in an airtight jar.

Crisp top casseroled beef *page 77*   Kidney ragout *page 85*
Casserole of rabbit with juniper berries *page 97*

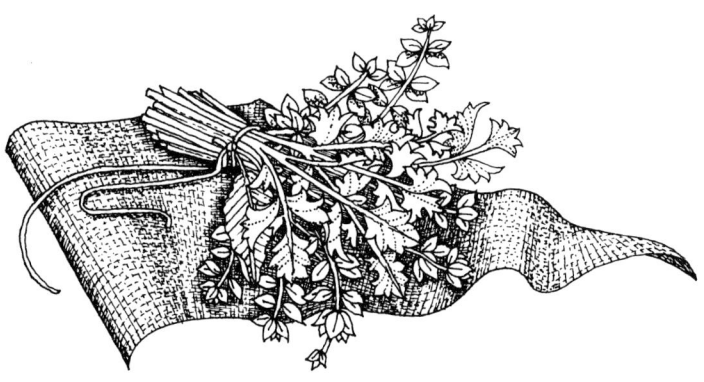

Burnet (*sanguisorba minor*)

Also called Salad Burnet. This was originally a Mediterranean plant that now grows widely in Britain. It has a nutty flavour with a touch of cucumber and goes excellently in salads, particularly in winter when it continues to flourish while other green things have gone to ground. It may also be used in soups and stews and with cheese, and it makes a good tisane. It is a small plant with lacy, intricate leaves but is in fact much tougher than it appears and will withstand most weather conditions. It produces reddish flowers and the plants should be cut back regularly to keep the leaves flourishing. In the sixteenth century it was thought that it quickened the spirit when infused in wine and it was also used as a protection against the plague and to staunch wounds.

Chamomile (*matricaria chamomilla*)

Not to be confused with the Roman or Lawn chamomile (anthemis nobilis), which is purely for gardening use when making a lawn. Chamomile has been known for centuries as a medicinal plant containing in its flowers a deep blue oil which is a strong healing substance. Chamomile is not used in cooking today, but a relaxing tisane can be made from the attractive blue flowers and an infusion of them will act as a lightening and conditioning rinse for fair hair. The plant is an annual grown from seed and is very easy to cultivate, making a good display when in flower. The flower heads should be picked when just in bloom and dried slowly in the airing cupboard or oven with the door ajar.

Chervil (*anthriscus cerifolium*)

Chervil is a subtle, slightly sweet flavoured herb that is much used in French cooking and often replaces parsley. It has the power of bringing out the flavour of other herbs when mixed with them, so is a constituent of *fines herbes* mixtures and also sometimes of a *bouquet garni*. Chervil also enhances the flavour of green vegetables and new potatoes and blends well with egg, cheese and chicken dishes. Chervil bears some resemblance to parsley but has a sweet scent that parsley lacks. It is an annual plant which must be grown from seed and the leaves are pale green. It should not be allowed to produce its small white flowers, but should be gathered and stored before they bloom. It grows well in tubs and window boxes, being one herb that does not like too much direct sunshine.

Avocado with herb dressing *page 66*
Chervil soup *page 71*
Cottage cheese and ham cocottes *page 74*
Lamb-kebabs *page 91*

Foil baked corn on the cob *page 111*
Asparagus with béarnaise sauce *page 117*
Rémoulade dressing *page 153*

Comfrey (*symphytum officinale*)

Comfrey is a great healing herb that features in many of today's herbal remedies. It is also known as Knitbone in rural areas and the herbalist Culpeper makes the somewhat hyperbolic claim that 'boiled with dissevered pieces of flesh in a pot, it will join them together again'. Be that as it may, it certainly is known to staunch bleeding cuts and help the healing of bruises. Comfrey grows quickly and easily and is much used as a green-manuring crop. The leaves have a slightly bitter flavour that is unusual when added to salads and it can also be eaten like spinach. The stalks taste good when cooked and eaten like asparagus. It grows to 70 or 100 cm (2 ft 6 in to 3 ft) and has a hairy stem and leaves. It prefers damp, darkish places like ditches and below walls and produces bell-shaped flowers in blue, purple, pink or cream.

Coriander (*coriandrum sativum*)
This is mainly used as a spice (see page 44) but the young leaves are tasty and interestingly flavoured and go well in soups and salads. It grows here in sunny spots and has feathery leaves and pinkish flowers. The plant itself smells rather unpleasant until the fruits begin to ripen and their aroma is the one that you then notice.

Cucumber à la grecque *page 67*

Marinaded mushrooms *page 68*

Barbecued spare ribs *page 79*

Crumb topped pork chops *page 80*

Gourmet mushrooms *page 116*

Costmary (*chrysanthem balsamita*)
This is also called Alecost or Bible Leaf since the pressed leaves were used to mark the place in family Bibles. It is very easy to grow and should always be used fresh. The leaves have a minty scent and a lemon flavour which intensifies the flavour of the ingredients used with it. They make a good flavouring for most dishes and are used in herbal teas and *pot pourris*. Costmary grows well in most soils provided there is some sun, and reaches about 70 cm (2 ft 6 in) in height with long thin leaves and white and yellow flowers. The roots, like those of mint and balm, tend to spread so costmary should be grown in places where its creeping won't damage more delicate plants.

Dandelion (*taraxacum officinale*)
This is mainly thought of as a common British weed but is in fact a very nutritious plant. Dandelion juice has considerable healing powers. The leaves may be eaten raw in salads or cooked like spinach, the roots can be dried and ground up to make dandelion coffee and the flowers make an excellent country wine. The French cultivate dandelions as a specific vegetable which is sold in shops and markets. When used raw the leaves are best blanched briefly, particularly if they have been gathered from a field or hedgerow. Dandelion is a perennial plant that is difficult to uproot once it has become established. The tooth-shaped leaves gave it the original French name *dent de lion* which became

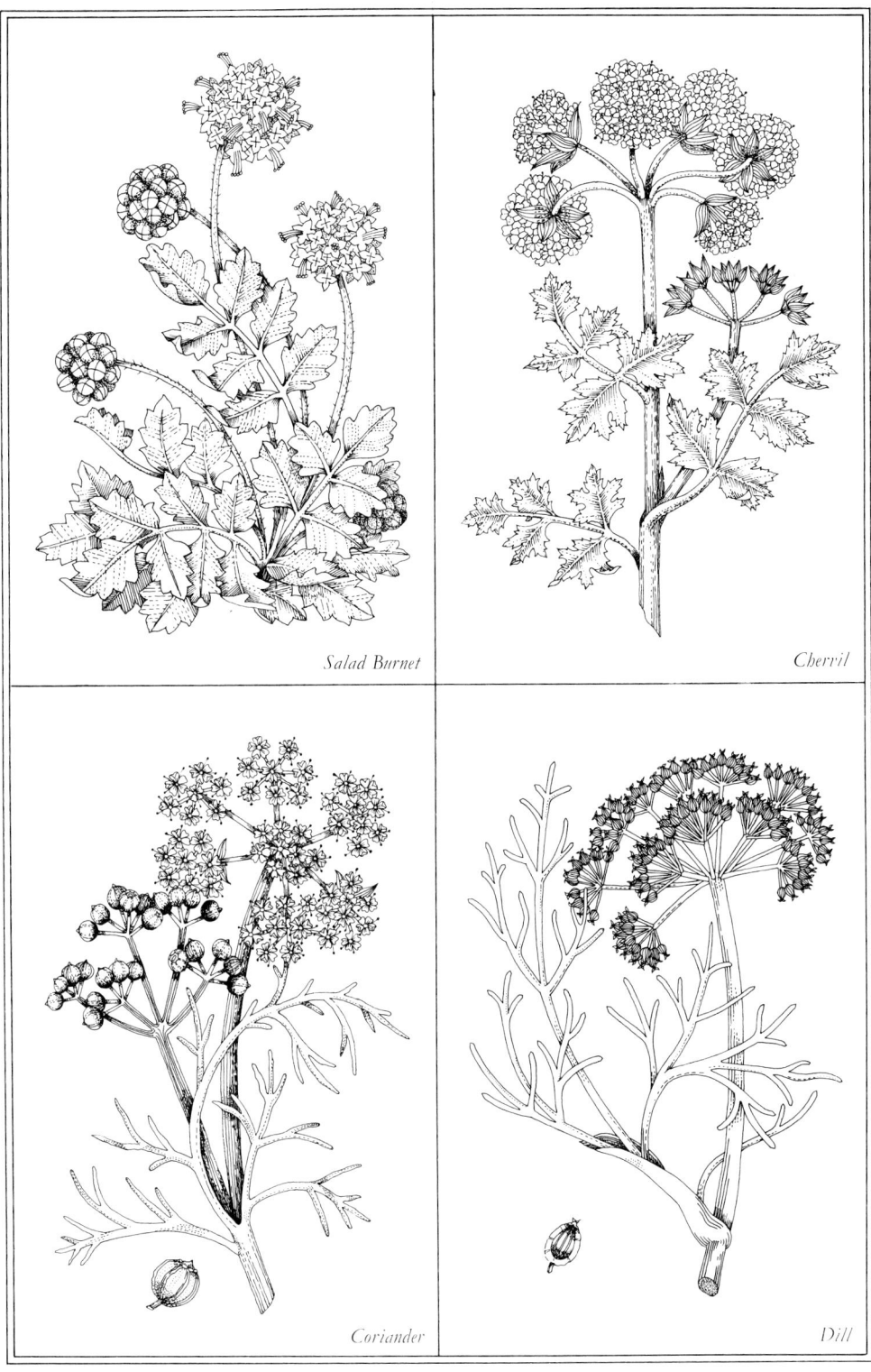

Salad Burnet

Chervil

Coriander

Dill

corrupted and anglicised. The bright yellow flowers have masses of slim petals which turn into the well-known dandelion clock seed heads which re-seed the plants copiously from year to year.

Dill (*peucedanum graveolens*)

Dill is used about equally as a herb and a spice (see page 45). When grown in the garden it should be kept away from fennel as the two plants, although in some ways similar, can affect the flavours of each other and there is also the risk that cross-pollination may occur, producing a bastard plant. Dill has a piquant flavour and digestive properties. Use the leaves with cucumber, in salads, with cooked green vegetables and sprinkled on new potatoes. Dill is a member of the same family as parsley and has a dark green stem flecked with blue and feathery blue-green leaves. The flowers are flattish and yellow.

Cream of fish soup *page 72*	Carrot with dill cream sauce *page 110*
Boiled lamb with dill sauce *page 82*	Dill cream dressing *page 153*

Fennel (*foeniculum vulgare*)

This is also used both as a herb and a spice (see page 45). Fennel has attracted a lot of superstition through the ages. The Greeks saw it as a symbol of success and called it 'Marathon' after their victory there. The old herbalists claimed that it increased a mother's milk, cured anyone who had eaten poisonous mushrooms, improved the complexion after illness and acted as an aid to slimming. This last was probably because of its digestive properties which are still recognised today. The slightly anise flavour marries well with fish and is especially good with oily fish which tends to be indigestible. Try it also in marinades, soups, sauces and salads. Fennel grows fairly tall and, like dill, has feathery foliage and flattish yellow flowers. It is a hardy plant that is often found growing wild in south-west England and although it likes sun it will grow in tubs or window boxes.

Cucumber à la grecque *page 67*	Cream of fish soup *page 72*
Seafood cocktail *page 69*	Swedish herring salad *page 124*

Fines herbes

Classically this is a mixture of finely chopped leaves of chives, chervil, parsley and tarragon. Together these make a delicate flavouring for filling omelettes, sprinkling on fish and poultry dishes and in salads. If making your own *fines herbes* mixture from fresh or dried herbs use equal quantities of all four.

Roast loin of pork *page 78*	Artichokes with herb butter sauce *page 117*
Steak with *fines herbes* *page 90*	Chicory and orange salad *page 125*
Herb omelette *page 101*	Cheese dip *page 156*

Horseradish (*cochlearia armoracia*)

This is the root of a member of the mustard family. It can be grown in this country but the seeds rarely ripen so need to be purchased commercially for home growing from year to year. Horseradish has strong antibiotic properties and is also rich in vitamin C. It has a hot, biting, pungent taste and should be eaten raw. It is claimed that it stimulates the appetite. Because of its strength horseradish is best grated or cut into julienne strips and made into a dressing for salads or a cream to serve with roast beef and other meats. Horseradish grows fairly tall with large, shiny dark leaves, white flowers and eventually if they ripen, round seed pods.

Mackerel with horseradish cream *page 67*   Spicy tomato sauce *page 102*

Hyssop (*hyssopus officinalis*)

Hyssop is a very strong herb that should be used sparingly. The sixteenth century herbalists claimed that hyssop cured worms in children and also purged the insides, but felt it inadvisable that it should be taken without prescription by a qualified surgeon! The flowers and young shoots are edible and go well in soups and salads. Hyssop aids the digestion of fats, so it is helpful with rich and

Fennel   *Marjoram*

oily dishes. It is an ingredient of the liqueur Chartreuse. It grows to 70 or 100 cm (2 ft 6 in to 3 ft) high with dark green, slim, pointed leaves and small blue flowers set in the leaf angles. The whole plant smells fairly strong and grows almost anywhere. The leaves and flowers should be gathered as soon as blooming begins.

Lovage (*ligusticum scoticum*)

This is a therapeutic herb used through the ages for a variety of ills. It has a sharp, spicy flavour and is not widely used in cooking here, though popular in continental Europe. It was much used in the fifteenth century as a remedy for sick cattle. The leaves make a tasty lovage soup, and go well in all savoury dishes and add an extra meaty flavour to stews. It grows very tall, with dark shiny leaves and yellow flowers. Lovage takes about four years to reach its maximum height and is then useful for protecting lower growing plants.

Marjoram (*origanum majorana*)

Sweet marjoram has a spicy, slightly sweet taste that does not mask other delicate flavours. It has been known for years as a preservative and disinfectant. Use it in all delicately flavoured dishes and especially rubbed into roasts and in stuffings. Marjoram in this country does not care for cold winters. Its seeds rarely ripen. It grows low and bushy and has a strong fragrance and small greyish leaves. The flowers are white or mauve-white.

Beef olives *page 76*
Steak and mushroom pie *page 78*
Pork with herbs in cider *page 79*
Casserole of ox heart *page 84*
Liver in savoury sauce *page 86*
Chicken with fresh peaches in barbecue sauce
  page 95

Herb omelette *page 101*
Bacon and egg pie *page 103*
Lasagne al forno *page 108*
Avocado rice salad *page 120*

Mint

Mint comes from a huge family. The most widely known culinary varieties are *mentha viridis* (spearmint), *mentha piperita* (peppermint) and *mentha rotundi folia* (apple/Bowles mint). Mint came originally from the East and is still widely drunk as a herbal tea there. It was used here both as a strewing and a medicinal herb, while as early as the sixth century it was employed for cleaning teeth. Mint stimulates the appetite and is used classically in Britain as a sauce or jelly accompanying roast lamb. It is also cooked with potatoes, carrots and peas. It grows easily and rampantly and to prevent its creeping root system taking over the garden is best planted in a bottomless box or bucket. All mints are perennial and produce small flowers in pink, white or mauve. Spearmint has narrow pointed leaves, peppermint has long hairy leaves with a touch of red in

Melon and ginger cocktail; Prawns in soured cream sauce; ▶
Cucumber à la grecque

them while applemint has large round, slightly woolly leaves. The mints should not be grown near each other or cross-flavouring may occur. The plants should be cut back from time to time to prevent them getting too tall.

Mixed herbs

This is an all-purpose herb blend for seasoning in a hurry. The usual ingredients are parsley, sage, thyme, marjoram and tarragon. It goes well with all savoury dishes and makes a handy kitchen standby for those days when you don't want to brood on and measure an individual herb flavouring agent.

Oregano (*origanum vulgaris*)

This is a member of the marjoram family with, perhaps, a slightly more pungent flavour and aroma. The variety known as dittany of Crete was reckoned to be a powerful love potion. Oregano is widely used in Italian cooking, for pasta dishes and pizza and also with tomatoes. It may also be used in well flavoured stews. It is possible to grow oregano here but not really worth it since the flavour and aroma develop only in warm climates and the plant needs lots of sun to produce the spicy flavour that distinguishes it from the other marjorams.

Parsley (*petroselinum crispum* and *petroselinum sativum*)

The curly and Hamburg parsley varieties are valuable and versatile herbs. The

Apricot stuffed lamb with rosemary;
Sunshine carrots

curly parsley is the variety most commonly grown in Britain, while the Hamburg is more popular in continental Europe, where the roots also are eaten. The parsley plant has many legends attached to it, partly because of the length of time (often up to six weeks) that it takes the seeds to germinate. Superstition has it that during that time they go to the devil and back seven times. It is also said that parsley will only grow in households where the women wear the trousers and that it brings ill-luck if you transplant it. Extra good luck comes if you plant the seeds on Good Friday. The Greeks saw parsley as a symbol of death while the Romans wore wreaths of it at their feasts in order to prevent intoxication.

Most of the flavour of parsley lies in its stalks but the leaves are very attractive and the sprigs make a pretty garnish. Parsley, like chervil, brings out the flavour of other herbs so is always found in *bouquets garnis* and *fines herbes* mixtures. With fish a parsley sauce is delicious. Parsley is a biennial plant that may grow for a further season but will be lacking in flavour. It is fairly low-growing, with dark green curly leaves. Once the plant flowers it will go to seed and become useless so the flower stalks should be cut off to prevent this. The foliage should be cut regularly to promote new growth.

Purslane (*portulacca oleracea*)

Purslane contains vitamins, minerals and essential trace elements to provide excellent food value. It is a fairly rare herb these days so you usually have to grow it yourself to obtain it. It is easy and quick to grow, with thickish leaves and small yellow flowers. Both the leaves and young shoots are edible. The leaves can be added to salads and may also be used to bring out the flavour of other herbs. The shoots should be cooked and eaten like asparagus. Purslane also makes a good herbal tea.

Rosemary (*rosmarinus officinalis*)

Rosemary is supposed to grow only in the gardens of the righteous. Rosemary was thought to strengthen the memory and so became the symbol of remembrance and fidelity. It has a strong taste that overpowers other herbs, so it is best used on its own to enhance meat, fish or poultry dishes. Rosemary is a tall growing shrub that is difficult to start from seed. You can buy a small bush from a nursery or take a cutting from an established one. Rather than leaves, it has dark green shiny needles like a pine tree and produces white or blue small flowers. Care should be taken not to let frost get at the bush until it is well settled in its final growing place.

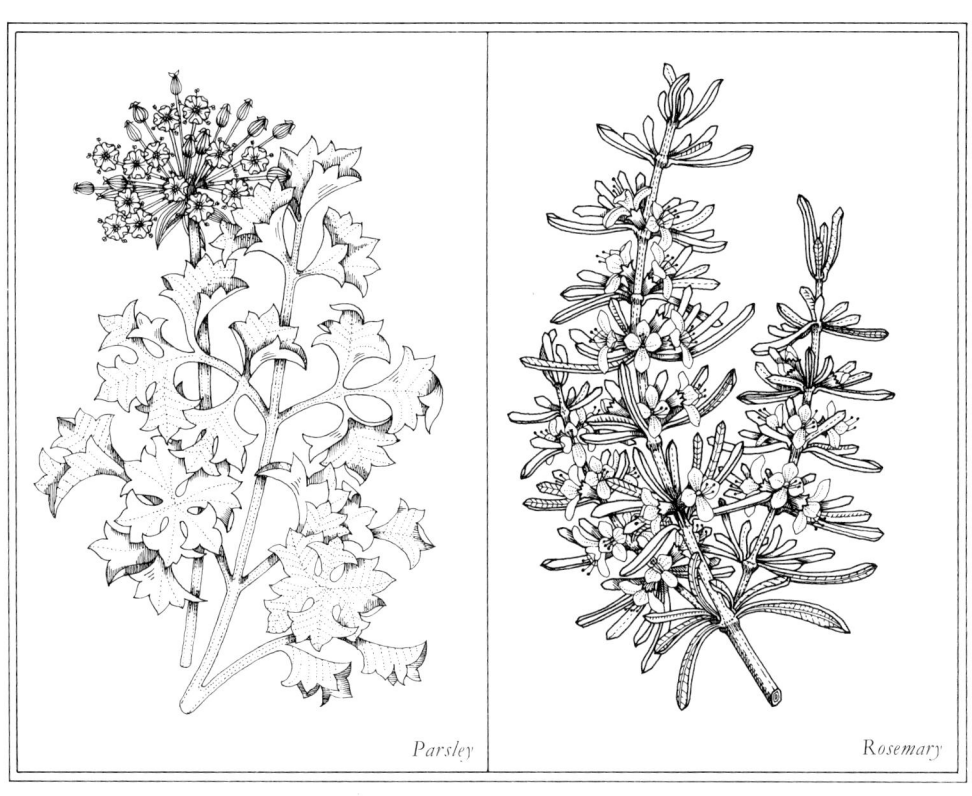

Parsley   *Rosemary*

Rue *(ruta graveolens)*

Also called the Herb of Grace, this is still cultivated for its bitter oil for medicinal purposes and was thought to act as a protection against germs. Judges carried it in their posies to ward off the infections of the courtroom. The strong bitter flavour adds an unusual touch to salads. The leaves should be used fresh. Rue grows to medium height and flourishes even in poor soil provided there is enough sun. It has small, branching, bluish-green leaves and little yellow flowers.

Sage *(salvia officinalis)*

A powerful healing herb, sage was used by the Greeks and Romans as an antidote to snakebite. It has a pungent, slightly bitter flavour that is well set off in fatty dishes. Sage is good in stuffings, casseroles, salads and with cheese. It grows easily to 70 or 100 cm (2 ft 6 in or 3 ft) high, with slightly hairy, grey-green leaves and pale blue or mauve flowers in its second year. It is a perennial plant but tends to become woody after about four years so should then be replaced. Cut it frequently to maintain bushy growth.

Roast loin of pork *page 78*

Pork stroganoff *page 90*
Saltimbocca *page 94*
Duckling, apple and celery casserole *page 96*

Sage and onion stuffing *page 155*
Herb bread *page 156*
Herb croûtons *page 156*

Savory *(satureia hortensis* and *satureia montana)*

Summer and winter savory give fresh herbs all year round. The summer savory is strong with a slightly peppery flavour and is known in continental Europe as the 'bean herb' because of its power to bring out flavour in all kinds of beans without leaving any taste of its own. The winter variety is also peppery and both types are good with indigestible dishes such as pork. Summer savory is a sun-loving annual with infrequent groups of narrow thickish leaves. The flowers are white or mauve and grow in clusters of five at the leaf angles. Winter savory looks fairly like the summer variety but has white or blue flowers and is a perennial.

Sorrel *(rumex scutatus)*

French and garden sorrel grow in this country but the French type has the better flavour. It makes a good spring green cooked on its own and also a soup. The sourish tangy flavour makes the raw leaves useful in salads and with egg dishes. Sorrel grows easily in this country although the variety most commonly found in our hedges and ditches is the less well-flavoured garden variety. French sorrel grows fairly tall with wide leaves and reddish spikes of small flowers, which

Sage

Summer savory

should be cut back to stop the plant going to seed. Sorrel becomes woody after about four years and plants should then be replaced.

Sweet cicely (*myrrhis odorata*)
The leaves have a slight anise flavour and sweet cicely is, as its name implies, a sweetening herb similar to angelica. Cook it with tart fruit such as rhubarb or apple and there is no need to use sugar – useful for slimmers and diabetics. It flourishes from spring until autumn so can be used fresh virtually all year round. Sweet cicely is a perennial plant that grows fairly tall. It has a hollow stem and large feathery leaves and produces clusters of white flowers. The flowers should be cut off to keep the leaves flourishing.

Tarragon (*artemisia dracunculus*)
Tarragon has an unusual, original flavour and is a vital ingredient in bearnaise, tartare and hollandaise sauces. It is strong, so should be used sparingly. It is always found in *fines herbes* mixtures, is a good flavouring for poultry, seafood and other delicate dishes and excellent in salads. The French variety (which is much better for cooking than its Russian counterpart) is grown from

rootstock cuttings and likes sun and well-drained soil. After a few years the plant will become weak so further root cuttings should be taken from it and planted. It grows quite tall and has shiny leaves and white clusters of flowers which will not grow much beyond the bud stage in a cool summer.

Thyme (*thymus vulgaris* and *thymus citriodorus*)

There are over a hundred varieties of thyme of which the garden and lemon types are those most commonly used in cooking. Both aid digestion and also have antiseptic properties, so were used as strewing herbs and also in the posies carried to ward off infection. Thyme is used in a wide variety of savoury dishes and is one of the basic herbs in a *bouquet garni*. Lemon thyme adds a hint of lemon to stuffings and poultry dishes. Thyme is a low-growing perennial plant that develops as a spreading bush. The garden thyme has small leaves and mauve flowers, while lemon thyme has broader leaves. Both can be grown from seeds or cuttings and the bushes should be replaced every few years when they start to lose their fragrance. While they flourish the plants should be cut back regularly to maintain vigorous growth.

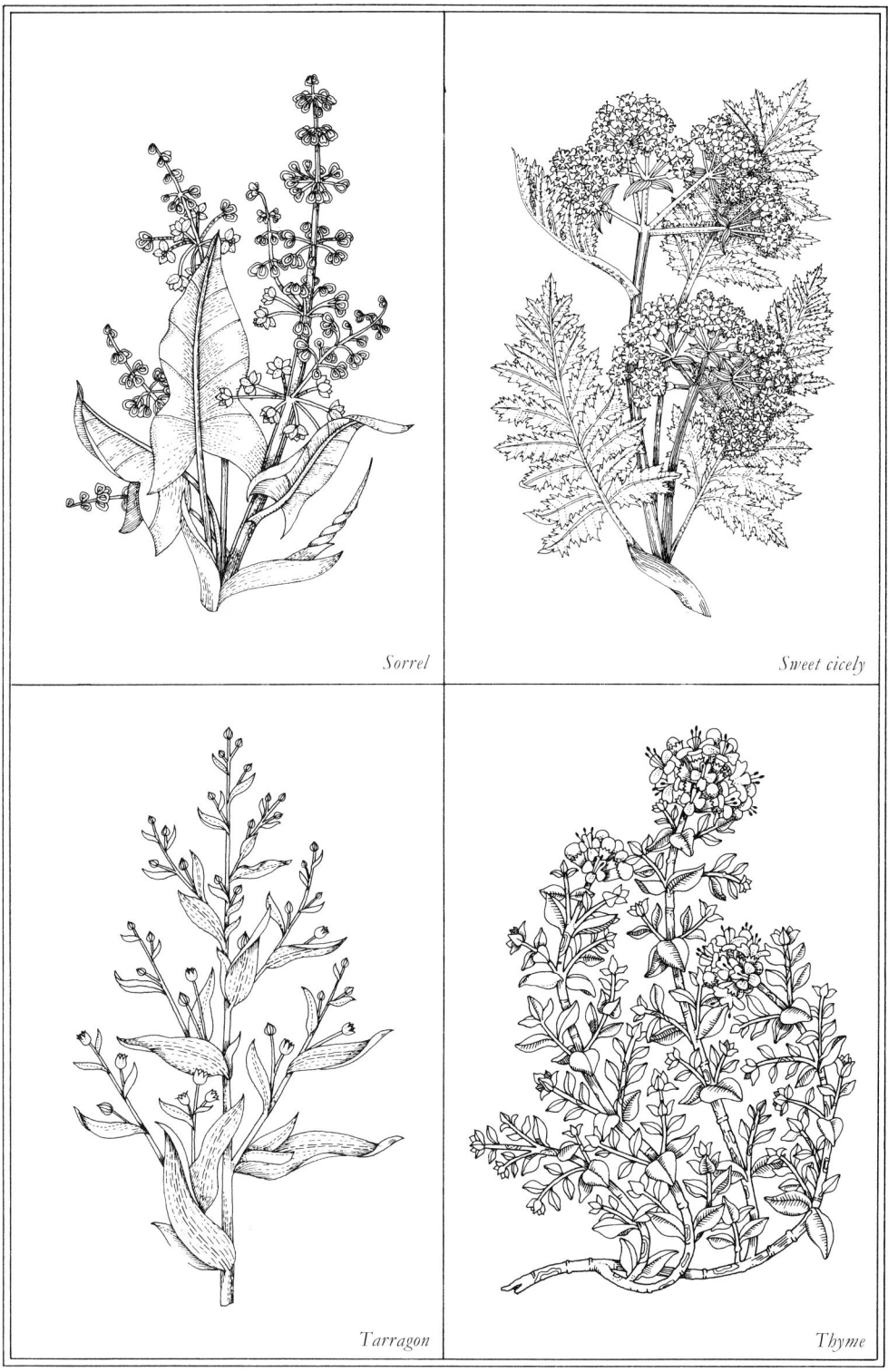

Sorrel

Sweet cicely

Tarragon

Thyme

Spices and Other Seasonings

Allspice (*pimenta officinalis*)
Also known as Jamaica Pepper and Pimento although it is no relation to the sweet red peppers (capsicum) which are also called pimento or pimiento in this country.

In spite of its name, allspice is not a mixture of spices but the berries of the allspice tree. The name comes from their flavour which is reminiscent of combined cloves, cinnamon and nutmeg. It is sold both whole and ready-ground and the whole berries are included in pickling spice. Allspice is used in marinades, meat, fish and curry dishes where a spicy flavour is sought. It's also used in Christmas pudding and is found in Bénédictine and Chartreuse liqueurs. It was a major ingredient of the Elizabethan *pot pourri* mixtures. Allspice grows in tropical climates, mainly in Jamaica.

Danish meat balls *page 80*
Pickled meat *page 88*
Sweet and sour red cabbage *page 115*
Creamed rice amontillado *page 137*

Sultana and cherry spice cake *page 144*
Spiced apples *page 155*
Spiced prunes *page 155*

Anise (*pimpinella anisum*)
Also known as aniseed. The seeds themselves are the spice though the young leaves are sometimes used as a herb (see page 22). Anise aids digestion and forms the basis of alcoholic drinks such as Pernod, Ricard and Anisette (all French), the Greek Ouzo and Turkish Raki. Aniseed sweets are perennially popular with children and the distinctive odour acts as a lure to many animals. In drag hunting, a sack soaked in aniseed oil is used to lay the trail for hounds to follow. Anise is used mainly to flavour cakes and biscuits and the anise-based drinks mentioned may be used sparingly for an unusual touch in sauces for fish and in certain soups.

Aniseed biscuits *page 144*

Caper (*capparis spinosa*)
The flower buds of the caper bush are always sold pickled in wine vinegar. They have a powerful aromatic taste which is fully developed only after they are pickled; care should be taken not to allow the pickling liquid to dry out once the

jar has been opened and some of the capers used. Capers are traditionally served in England in a sauce with boiled mutton and are also an ingredient of sauce tartare. They make an interesting addition to other meat, fish and seafood dishes and also form an attractive garnish. The caper bush is a tropical plant whose flowers, if allowed to open, bloom for just one day. You should not pickle the caper spurge (euphorbia lathyrus) growing in your garden as it is poisonous.

Caraway (seed of the *carum carvi*)

This is one of the oldest spices known to Europe and much used in central European and Jewish cookery today. Caraway seeds have a spicy, slightly liquorice-like, rather sharp taste and are used for flavouring cakes, biscuits and bread and added to soups and stews. It is an ingredient of the liqueur Kummel and, like anise, caraway aids digestion. Swiss cheese fondues are sometimes flavoured with caraway and it makes a tasty addition to home-made or bought cream cheese, or sprinkled into cabbage.

Veal goulash with caraway dumplings *page 93*   Rainbow coleslaw *page 122*

Cabbage with caraway *page 115*   Caraway cobbler ring cake *page 142*

Cardamom (*elletaria cardamomum*)

Cardamom is a member of the ginger family, and the seeds form the spice. The Egyptians chewed them to whiten their teeth and today they're widely used in Eastern and continental European cooking. Their flavour is strong and spicy with a hint of lemon. Cardamom is the second most expensive spice (saffron being the first) because the seed pods have to be individually snipped from the plant with scissors. It is an ingredient of most curry powders and used for flavouring both sweet and savoury dishes. It is used in Christmas cakes and puddings, spicy sweet dishes and fruit salads, rice pudding, ginger-bread and some sausage dishes.

Spicy red curry *page 85*

Citrus spice salad *page 120*

Fresh fruit salad with honey *page 135*

Swedish cardamom cake *page 148*

Cardamom

Cayenne (*capsicum frutescens*)

Cayenne is a bitingly hot, slightly sweetish spice from the red pepper (capsicum) family. It is always sold ground as a brownish-red powder and adds zip to cheese sauce and cheese pastry or straws. It is also good sprinkled on sardines, fish pâtés and with seafood. Cayenne is an essential ingredient of barbecue sauce and devilled dishes. It has digestive properties and is rich in vitamin C, but must be used sparingly or it can make a dish uneatable.

Chili con carne *page 76*

West Indian lamb *page 92*

Lamb kebabs *page 91*

Cheese and parsley soufflé *page 101*

Golden sauté potatoes *page 113*

Ratatouille layered pudding *page 113*

Parsley butter *page 153*

Indian chutney *page 154*

Celery seed (*apium graveolens*)

These are seeds of a different plant from the celery that we normally eat as a vegetable. These seeds have a strong distinctive taste which does, nonetheless, resemble celery in some respects and they add bite in both flavour and texture to soups and stews. Celery seed is also found in several seasoning blends (see page 52).

Barbecued lamb chops *page 82*

Rainbow coleslaw *page 122*

Chili

Chili also comes from the capsicum family and is subject to a wide variety of spellings, the most common alternatives being chilly, chile and chilli. These red peppers range through degrees of hotness from sweet and mild to stinging and fiery. Ground chili is extremely hot so use it very sparingly. The pre-mixed commercial powders sold as chili usually contain cumin, oregano, garlic, cloves, allspice and salt plus the *chilli ancho*, a not-too-hot capsicum variety. Use chili powder in Mexican dishes such as chili con carne, to pep up baked beans and also in chutneys and ketchups.

Chili con carne *page 76*

Barbecued lamb chops *page 82*

Spicy red curry *page 85*

Seafood creole *page 87*

Chicken with fresh peaches in barbecue sauce *page 95*

Devilled grilled turkey *page 96*

Spaghetti bolognese *page 100*

Spicy tomato sauce *page 102*

Ham and brown rice salad with fruit *page 121*

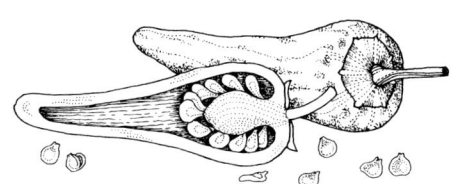

Chili

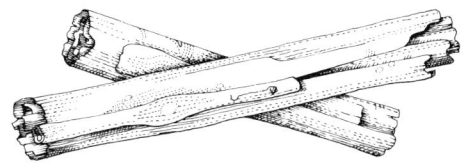

Cinnamon

Cinnamon *(*the bark of the *cinnamomum zeylanicum* tree*)*
The tree is a member of the laurel family. The best quality cinnamon is grown in Sri Lanka and is sold in both ground and stick form. Cinnamon is best used ground for general cooking in cakes and puddings, as a flavouring for chocolate dishes and on cheesecake and pork dishes. It is also good in hot drinks for colds and sore throats. Stick cinnamon is best for infusing in hot drinks or in mulled wine and punches. Cinnamon is widely used in all sweet, spicy baking.

Cloves *(eugenia caryophyllata)*
Cloves are the flower bud of this shrub and come mainly from Zanzibar. Their name comes from the Latin 'clovus', a nail, because of their nail shape. You

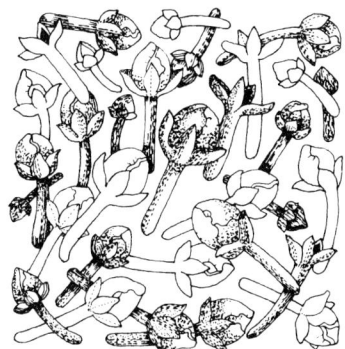

Cloves

can buy them whole or ground and their main cookery uses are in apple dishes, bread sauce, Christmas pudding and mincemeat. They are also good for flavouring marinades for meat and fish, studded directly into ham and for pickles and mulled wine. Oil of cloves is a standard remedy for toothache and cloves are also used to make pomanders.

Easy tomato soup *page 70*

Spiced silverside *page 76*
Steak and mushroom pie *page 78*
Barbecued spare ribs *page 79*
Spicy red curry *page 85*

Sugar glazed gammon *page 91*

Citrus spice salad *page 120*
Chicken and rice salad *page 121*

Apple and fig pie *page 128*
Pears and orange pancakes *page 131*

Spotted Dick *page 132*
Pumpkin chiffon pie *page 133*
Dried fruit compote *page 136*
Spiced pears *page 136*

Raisin streusel cake *page 140*
Ginger snaps *page 140*

Spiced apples *page 155*
Spiced prunes *page 155*
Spicy fruit punch *page 157*
Glühwein *page 157*
Spiced cider punch *page 157*

Coriander (*coriandrum sativum*)

The seeds of this plant form the coriander spice but the young leaves may be used as a herb (see page 28). The flavour is spicy, sweet and orangey though fairly mild. Coriander is found whole in pickling spice, ground in pickles, chutney and commercial curry powders. It is a very good flavouring for meat dishes and in Elizabethan times was rubbed into uncooked meat to act as a preservative. You can grow coriander in the south of England though it really prefers hotter climes. You are unlikely to get enough seed off it to make it worthwhile without giving up quite a lot of ground.

Cucumber à la grecque *page 67*
Marinaded mushrooms *page 68*

Barbecued spare ribs *page 79*

Crumb topped pork chops *page 80*

Gourmet mushrooms *page 116*

Cumin (*cuminum cyminum*)

These seeds are strong, spicy and slightly bitter. They are widely used in Eastern cookery and also found in commercial curry and chili powders. In the Middle Ages cumin was very popular in English cookery but by the eighteenth century it tended to be replaced by caraway in recipes. Cumin, like caraway, is an aid to digestion. Use it in kebabs, meat dishes, with chicken, lamb and vegetables.

Lamb kebabs *page 91*

Oriental carrots *page 110*

Curry powder

This is a blend of various spices. Purists like to mix and grind their own freshly for each curry but many of the commercial powders are very good, particularly after you have found one whose degree of hotness suits your palate. The spices are usually a selection of pepper, mustard, fenugreek, cayenne, cardamom, coriander, cumin, ginger and turmeric. A useful tip for using bought curry powder is to warm it slightly before adding it to the other ingredients – this brings out its flavour. Apart from its use in curries the powder may be added to sauces and soups for added zest.

Prawns in soured cream sauce *page 67*   Curried rice with spinach *page 115*

West Indian lamb *page 92*   Curried potato and frankfurter salad *page 123*
Devilled grilled turkey *page 96*

Dill (*peucedanum graveolens*)

The seeds of this plant are a spice while the leaves may be considered a herb (see page 30). Dill has good digestive properties and its piquant flavour makes it a useful seasoning for salt-free diets. Dill is much used in Scandinavia and in continental fish dishes and is good in pickles, with cucumber, salads and other vegetables.

Mackerel with horseradish cream *page 67*   Boiled lamb with dill sauce *page 82*
Seafood cocktail *page 69*

Fennel (*foeniculum vulgare*)

This again is a spice and herb plant (see page 30). Fennel has a stronger flavour than dill, with a touch of anise in it. It too has digestive properties and is good with hard-to-digest fatty foods such as oily fish. Other uses are in marinades, soups, sauces and salads.

Fenugreek (*trigonella foenum-graecum*)

The small, yellow-brown beans are used as a spice. Fenugreek has been used since very early times for cooking and medication and is in some places still cultivated for its medicinal properties. It is widely grown in areas where there is malnutrition as it has recognised body-building virtues and is cheap and heavy-cropping. Fenugreek is not widely known or used in English cooking but is found in commercial curry powders. Use it in chutneys and pickles where its slightly harsh hot flavour blends in.

Ginger (*zingiber officinale*)

The root of this plant has an unusual, hot, sweet taste and is sold crystallised, preserved in syrup, green, dried, whole or ground. It has been known in English cookery since before the Norman Conquest and was much used in mediaeval recipes for both its flavour and preservative qualities. Today it has numerous commercial applications in soft drinks such as ginger beer and ginger

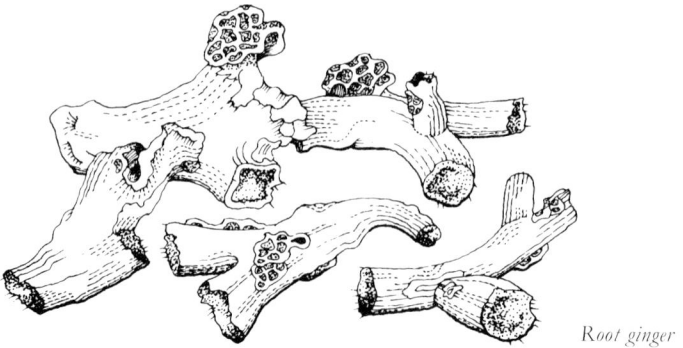

Root ginger

ale and is also an essential ingredient of gingerbread and ginger pudding. Its flavour marries well with chocolate, is good in curries and makes an excellent hot contrast when served with melon.

Juniper (*juniperus communis*)

This spice is the fruit of a shrub that is native to the British Isles. For many years it was considered a magic plant, woven about with superstition, and also a powerful protection against epidemics. The small black berries are aromatic, with a pine tang. For maximum flavour they should be crushed before adding to a dish. Juniper is a major flavouring agent in gin and is used when cooking venison, game (where it removes the 'gamey' taste that some people dislike) pâtés, sauerkraut and pork dishes.

Mace (*myristica fragrans*)

Mace is the outer covering of nutmeg, which is the fruit of the myristica fragrans tree. It is often sold powdered, as once the nutmeg kernel is removed mace becomes very hard and grinding is difficult at home. But you can buy blade mace which is useful for infusing. Mace is a traditional English spice used in mulls and punches and in potted meat and fish recipes. It is also good in béchamel sauce, meat loaf, stews, pies and some puddings. Oil of mace helps insomnia. Buy this spice in small quantities and use quickly as it does not keep its flavour well. If you have no mace, nutmeg can usually be substituted but a much smaller quantity is required.

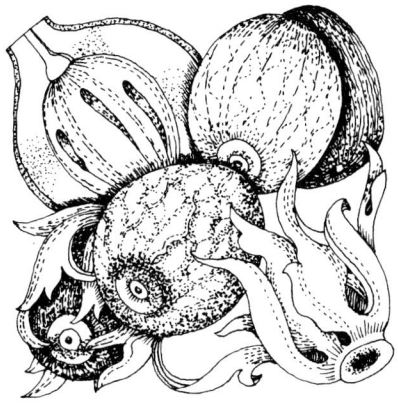

Mace and nutmeg

Potted shrimps *page 68*
Liver pâté *page 69*
Kipper pâté *page 69*

Cannelloni *page 103*
Fish cakes *page 105*
Chicken turnovers *page 106*

Baked courgettes with cream and almonds
  page 112

Stuffed mushrooms *page 116*

Chicken and rice salad *page 121*

Bramble syllabub *page 135*

Marmalade mace tea bread *page 143*
Sesame seed crescents *page 148*

Mixed spice

Blended specially for the English market, mixed spice is a combination of the most popular sweet baking spices such as cinnamon, cloves, nutmeg and allspice. Use it in fruit cakes, fruit puddings and general baking.

Potted shrimps *page 68*

Cherry strudel *page 129*
Plumb crumble *page 132*
Dried fruit compote *page 136*

Spicy scones *page 146*
Mandarin spice gâteau *page 149*

Spicy apricot stuffing *page 155*
Spicy fruit punch *page 157*

Mustard (*brassica nigra* and *brassica alba*)

Mustard is one of the oldest condiments known. It comes from the black or white seeds of the mustard plant. Black seeds give aroma and white ones pungency and most mustards are a combination of the two in varying proportions. The seeds are ground to make a mustard flour (except in certain blends like the

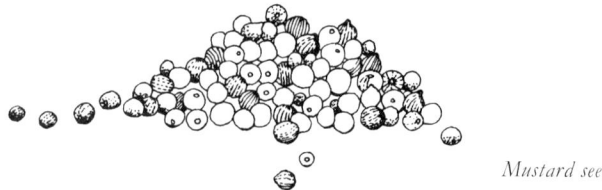

Mustard seed

French Moutarde de Meaux) and the special flavours that differentiate the various types are produced by the liquid which is used to moisten the flour. Most imported mustards come in paste form but the most popular one in this country is English dry mustard, grown here. Mustard goes well as a condiment with all traditional English food such as ham, steak and beef and is an essential ingredient in such dishes as Welsh Rarebit. French mustards are the best to use in salad dressings and sauces and those who like them can also buy mustards from Austria, Belgium, Germany and the U.S.A. fairly easily.

Cheese baked eggs *page 74*

Spiced silverside *page 76*
Barbecued spare ribs *page 79*
Rum-basted bacon *page 81*
Tangy chops *page 81*

Sugar glazed gammon *page 91*
Chicken with fresh peaches in barbecue sauce
   page 95
Devilled grilled turkey *page 96*

Spinach layer pie *page 100*
Chive sauce *page 105*

Zesty haddock *page 106*
Bacon burgers with parsley sauce *page 107*

Courgettes and tomatoes au gratin *page 112*

Bean sprout salad *page 120*
Ham and brown rice salad with fruit *page 121*
Ham roulades vinaigrette *page 122*
Tuna bean salad *page 123*

Piccalilli *page 154*
Indian chutney *page 154*

Nutmeg (*myristica fragrans* or *myristica officinalis*)

Nutmeg is a very powerful spice with a strong aroma that was used in the Middle Ages as a fumigant against the plague. Nutmeg was very popular with the English in the seventeenth to nineteenth centuries and many people carried it around with them, plus a small pocket grater, so that they could sprinkle a little into drinks and on their food. Nutmeg loses its scent quickly so should be stored carefully if you buy it ground. Whole nutmegs can be grated a little as and when needed. Nutmeg goes well in cheese sauce, soufflés, egg dishes and Christmas pudding and cake.

Jellied tomato rings with cottage cheese
   page 66
Easy tomato soup *page 70*

Beef olives *page 76*
Somerset tripe *page 85*

Spinach layer pie *page 100*
Cannelloni *page 103*
Bacon and egg pie *page 103*
Bacon burgers with parsley sauce *page 107*

Paprika (*capsicum annum*)

A sweet mild spice with an attractive reddish-brown colour, paprika is popular for a garnishing touch on pale egg and cheese dishes. Its keeping powers are very poor and it is one of the spices that should be bought little and often. The best paprika comes from Hungary and it is an essential ingredient in goulash. Some varieties are hotter than others.

Pepper (*piper nigrum*)

White pepper comes from the fully ripened berries of this tree. The outer skin is removed and the berries are cleaned. It can be bought whole or ground and is less pungent and aromatic than black pepper but good in light sauces as it does not discolour them. Black pepper comes from the berries picked while still green and left to dry in the sun until they shrivel and darken. It too is sold whole or ground and is at its best freshly milled. Green peppercorns are sold in cans. They are the unripe berries picked and canned without drying out. Their fresh pungent flavour is totally different from the dried varieties and adds an unusual tang to grilled meat or poultry. They can also be mashed for sauces.

Most savoury recipes are seasoned with a little pepper; the recipes mentioned here are those in which pepper is a major flavouring ingredient.

Pickling spice

A peculiarly English blend, pickling spice is usually made up of mustard seed, coriander, allspice, chilies and ginger, which are not ground. It should be used as a flavouring rather than an ingredient in chutneys and pickled fruits and vegetables and the best method is to tie the required quantity in a muslin bag on the end of a piece of string so it can be removed easily when it has done its duty.

Pickled cider herrings *page 68*

Poppy seed (*papaver somniferum*)

This is the opium poppy but the seeds do not contain the drug. They have a nutty flavour and are widely used in Jewish and central European cookery. Poppy seeds are very hard when dry and virtually impossible to grind satisfactorily at home, so you should buy them in the form in which you wish to use them. The whole seeds taste and look good sprinkled on bread, rolls and biscuits, while ground they make a flavouring for cakes and puddings. Poppy seed is often an ingredient of commercial curry powders.

Broad beans with poppy seeds *page 111*   Poppy seed yeast cake *page 141*

Saffron (*crocus sativus*)

The dried stigma of the autumn flowering crocus are the most expensive spice in the world, and said to be worth almost their weight in gold. Saffron is a very strong spice that gives flavour, scent and colour to dishes. It grew in great quantities at Saffron Walden in Essex in the sixteenth century but is now all

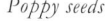

Poppy seeds

Saffron

imported. Because it is so expensive it is really worth buying only for those dishes where all three of its properties are needed. For adding a yellow colour to a pilaff or risotto a small quantity of turmeric makes a very adequate substitute. Real saffron is best saved for Cornish saffron cake and fish soups, such as bouillabaisse, or paella, where its distinctive flavour genuinely adds to the dish. Saffron can be bought both whole and ground.

Sesame seed (*sesamum indicum*)

This is widely used in Eastern cookery, especially on bread, cakes and biscuits, and sesame oil is used in the East for cooking. The seeds are also good in salads and sprinkled on cottage or cream cheese. Sesame seeds have a sweet, slightly burnt flavour which can be heightened by toasting them before use.

Sesame seeds

Thousand islands seafood salad *page 122*   Sesame seed crescents *page 148*

Sesame seed and almond flan *page 129*

Turmeric (*curcuma longa*)

Turmeric is the root of this plant, a member of the ginger family. It is used a great deal in Moroccan and Indian cookery and, although hot, is much milder than curry powder of which it is often a constituent. It is also added to mustard powder. In addition to flavouring, turmeric can be used to colour rice and other pale dishes an attractive yellow colour.

Spicy red curry *page 85*   Ham roulades vinaigrette *page 122*

West Indian lamb *page 92*   Piccalilli *page 154*
Golden sauté potatoes *page 113*

Vanilla (*vanilla planifolia*)

The pods of this climbing orchid are grown mainly in Mexico and France. Vanilla is a unique flavouring agent which resembles no other. You can buy it as an essence of which only a few drops are needed at a time, or buy whole pods which can be used several times. Leave a pod in the caster sugar jar and it will impart flavour over a long period of time. Vanilla marries well with chocolate dishes and also flavours custards and ice cream.

Spice doughnuts *page 146*

Vanilla

Other Seasonings

Salt is not a spice at all but a mineral. It is nonetheless an essential condiment in all cooking and one that is often combined with spices for extra seasoning power (see below). Sea salt and bay salt come from the sea – rock salt is mined or pumped up from salt beds. Coarse salt is stronger than the more common free-flowing variety. Table salts have magnesium carbonate added to help them run more freely.

Most savoury recipes are seasoned with a little salt. Salt, is however, a major ingredient in several pickles such as:

Pickled meat *page 88*   Piccalilli *page 154*

Monosodium glutamate This is a mineral which brings out the flavours in all kinds of food without leaving any savour of its own. It is used frequently in commercially prepared convenience foods such as dried soups, instant stocks and other ready mixed foods. It is also available for kitchen use but is usually mixed with other herbs or spices, as in the seasonings mentioned below.

Spice manufacturers often produce special seasoning blends in addition to their individual herbs and spices. These are intended to help cooks in a hurry and the spices or herbs have been mixed together in suitable proportions for flavouring particular dishes. Our recipes include several savoury seasoning blends and one sweet one, apple pie spice; this, as its name implies, is used to give a tang to apple and other fruit pies and pastries. It includes cinnamon, cloves, nutmeg or mace, allspice and ginger.

The savoury seasoning blends always include salt and pepper so you should avoid these or use them sparingly when preparing the basic ingredients. Most blends are based on monosodium glutamate and they include the relevant herbs and spices for the foods they are intended to accompany.

Barbecue seasoning includes chilies, cumin, garlic, cloves, paprika, salt and sugar. Use it as a base for barbecue sauce or to give an unusual fillip to salad dressings or plain stews.

Barbecued spare ribs *page 79*　　　　　　　Buttered swede *page 115*
Barbecued lamb chops *page 82*

Chicken seasoning contains no garlic but blended sage, thyme, marjoram and savory. Rub it on to a whole chicken or chicken pieces before roasting or grilling to give added brownness and flavour.

Chicken and tarragon soup *page 71*　　　　Italian chicken casserole *page 83*
　　　　　　　　　　　　　　　　　　　　Golden baked chicken joints *page 85*

Fish seasoning Garlic and other herbs lend distinction to even the plainest fish dish and this blend can be sprinkled straight on to fish before cooking, or added to an accompanying butter sauce.

Mackerel with horseradish cream *page 67*

Cream of fish soup *page 72*

Cod cutlets in mushroom cream sauce *page 87*

Lemon fish kebabs *page 97*

Swedish herring salad *page 124*

Italian seasoning omits Italy's beloved garlic but nonetheless gives authentic flavour to pizza and pasta dishes with its combination of oregano, basil, red pepper and rosemary.

Italian chicken casserole *page 83*

Cannelloni *page 103*

Ratatouille layered pudding *page 113*

Marinaded cauliflower and mushrooms *page 124*

Lamb seasoning has a touch of garlic, with rosemary and other lamb enhancing herbs, and can be used on chops and roasts and in casseroles and stuffings.

Mint lamb casserole *page 82*

Meat tenderiser This is not a seasoning at all, but is generally sold on the same counters. It is usually made from an enzyme called papain, obtained from the papaw fruit. It is particularly useful in shortening cooking times for tougher joints of meat. Many meat tenderisers are seasoned at least with salt and pepper.

Salad seasoning contains an unusual cheese flavour plus a slight touch of garlic. Add it to dressings or sprinkle directly on to salad ingredients.

Tuna bean salad *page 123*

Tossed fresh spinach salad *page 123*

Sandwich seasoning includes celery seed, sugar, paprika and garlic and is sprinkled on to the filling before the sandwich is closed.

Seasoning salt This is a very general seasoning, including salt, celery seed, sugar, paprika and garlic, for use in all types of savoury dishes.

Casseroled potatoes with parsnips *page 112*

Steak pepper and steak spice include salt, celery seed, pepper and onion and give a lift to plain grills.

Aromatics

While most herbs and some spices can lay claim to being aromatic we have, for the purpose of this book, taken the classification of an aromatic to include only the members of the onion family. All of these have been known since early civilisations both for their vegetable and medicinal uses. Today they are as popular as ever for culinary use and some are included in a number of herbal remedies.

Onion (*allium cepa*)

Onion is perhaps the queen of aromatics, with its diversity of uses and pungent, distinctive flavour and smell. Onions go well in soups, stews and sauces and can also be served as a separate vegetable or, chopped fine, with another vegetable such as peas. They may be eaten cooked or raw. The onions we eat in this country may be red, yellow, purple, green or white. Red are strongest and white have the most delicate flavour. Spanish onions are large and mild, English are smaller with more bite. Many people claim that an onion a day keeps coughs and colds away and the cut surface of an onion is also helpful in relieving the pain and swelling of a wasp or bee sting. Dried onion flakes are a useful store cupboard standby, to use in place of sliced onions; dried minced onion or onion salt will flavour sauces without adding texture.

Shallot (*allium ascalonicum*)

These look like onions but are much smaller and have brownish skins. Their flavour is mild and more subtle than that of an onion so they are good in salads and other dishes when used raw. Shallots are used a great deal in classic French recipes such as sauce béarnaise, beurre blanc and sauce Bercy.

Welsh onion (*allium fistulosum*)

These are grown mainly for their leaves, sometimes called 'onion green' or scallions. You rarely find them in shops though they are very easy to grow in a garden and flourish from spring through to autumn provided you keep cutting the leaves to encourage further growth. Welsh onions have no special connection with Wales – their name has developed from the Old English

Welsh onion

Chives

'wielisc', meaning foreign. Use them chopped as a delicate seasoning for salads, cream cheese and egg dishes.

Chives (*allium schoenoprasum*)

Also known in country districts as 'rush leek.' They will grow almost for ever in a garden as they seed themselves if left to flower and can also be divided at their bulb roots. Chives are best used uncooked as a seasoning or garnish for salads and other raw vegetables, or added at the last minute as an omelette filling or garnish for cheese soufflé.

Chives can be grown all year round if you bring them indoors in winter, and they are commercially freeze-dried with very successful results.

Garlic (*allium sativum*)

Garlic is one of the most powerful seasoning agents around and one that has been revered for centuries for culinary and medicinal use. In many very hot countries people eat garlic daily to prevent the development of such diseases as typhus and cholera. Garlic's essential volatile oil has strong antiseptic and anti-germ properties. To lessen the rather obtrusive flavour, a cut clove of garlic may be rubbed round a dish or rubbed on to meat and then discarded. For those who love it, the cloves should be chopped or crushed and added to the dish. Garlic may be used in any meat, fish or vegetable dish to good effect and can be bought all year round either in clove form or dried as garlic powder, garlic granules or garlic salt. In its dehydrated forms the smell is less strong and people who dislike it may prefer to use it this way. A cure for the smell of garlic on the breath is to eat some fresh parsley.

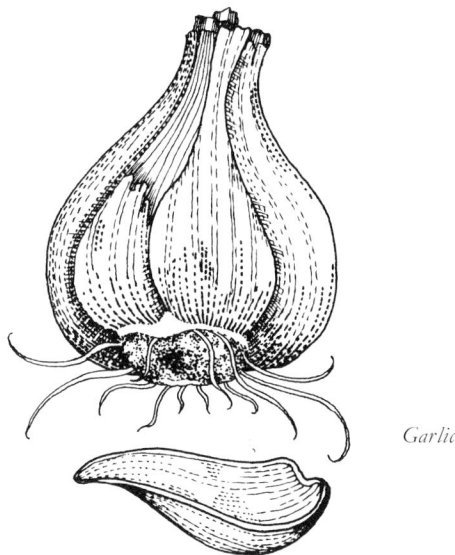

Garlic

Growing Your Own

You can grow herbs and some spices almost anywhere. They don't all need full sun all the time, although obviously those of Mediterranean origin are the better for it. They don't even need particulaly good soil; when you think how some plants scratch a living out of rocks in their native lands you can see that a nice cosy tub or window box will produce equally good results. All that is really important is good drainage.

In the garden

It is important to grow herbs so that they are easily accessible. You are less likely to be moved to rush out and gather a handful of parsley or chives if you have to put on wellingtons and walk over wet grass to reach them. Near the kitchen door is the classic place to grow herbs and cannot really be improved on.

A proper herb garden is obviously the best solution of all for the gardener-cook. Here you can grow the basics in sufficient quantity for your needs and also try out new herbs for experimenting. If you have the space, it is hard to beat the formal designs of the Elizabethan knot garden, where small intricate patterns of different herbs were grown individually surrounded by hedges of lavender, rosemary or low-growing box. Alternatively you can use paving stones to square off small beds for the different herbs. This has the advantage that you never have to walk on the soil to gather them. Growing them between the spokes of an old cart wheel is effective too, and takes up very little space.

If your garden is small you may be loth to give up much space for just growing herbs. But there is no reason why you cannot plant them along with

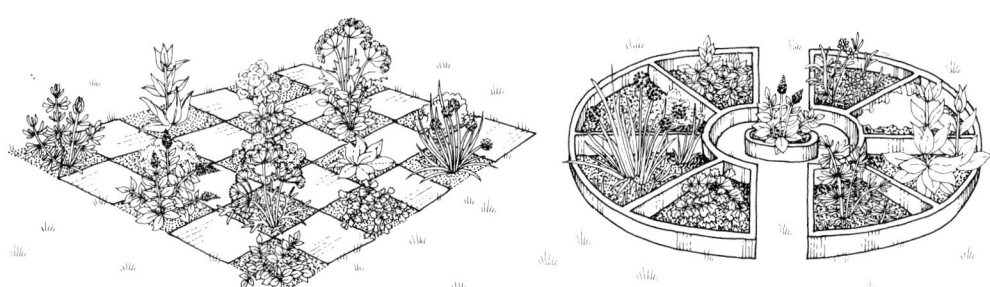

either flowers or vegetables in different spots around the garden. Some of the umbelliferous herbs such as fennel and dill are very attractive with their long feathery leaves and make an unusual addition to a flower bed. Some herbs can serve a dual purpose by helping the plants grown alongside. For instance, chives cultivated under an apple tree are said to prevent apple scab from forming and parsley helps roses to flourish and is also good beside tomatoes and asparagus. Lavender is said to assist the growth of all vegetables. Herbs such as balm attract bees (good for any garden) while caraway, anise and coriander each encourage the growth of the others.

Mint and balm have creeping root systems and can, if left to grow unchecked, gradually infiltrate the rest of the garden. For this reason it is best to start the plants off in a bottomless bucket or box sunk into the earth. This contains the roots and keeps the plants within reasonable bounds.

Herbs such as rosemary make good hedging after a few years and also give off a lovely scent if you brush past. A bay tree is very ornamental and can be grown somewhere you intended to plant a tree or bush anyway.

Indoor herbs

People without gardens can grow herbs indoors in pots or other containers. Many varieties that outdoors flourish only in summer will last all year round indoors. Remember, though, if there is central heating, that the plants will need frequent watering and a regular supply of fresh air. Popular herbs like chives and parsley grow particularly well indoors.

Starting herbs from scratch should be done from seeds in the case of annuals and cuttings in the case of perennials. It is also possible, though expensive, to buy the plants ready started from a nursery. Good seed packets carry full instructions for planting and care and most gardening books give information on looking after cuttings and small plants.

GARDENER'S CHART

Herb	Family/type	Grow from	Shape and height	Preferred soil	Cultivation
Angelica	Umbelliferae (biennial)	Seeds, root division	Tall, up to 2 m (6 ft)	Good, shady spot	Cut off flower heads to prevent copious reseeding
Anise	Umbelliferae (annual)	Seeds	Medium, about 60 cm (2 ft)	Light with lime, needs sun	Cut stems and allow to lie on the ground until fully ripe
Balm	Labiatae (perennial)	Seeds, cuttings	Medium, about 70 cm (2 ft 6 in)	Anywhere	Needs space for leaves to develop
Basil	Labiatae (annual)	Seeds	Medium, up to 1 m (3 ft)	Good, well-drained, needs sun	Pinch out tips to prevent flowering
Bay	Lauraceae (perennial)	Buy as a small established tree	Tall, up to 12 m (40 ft)	Good, needs sun	Watch out for frost when young
Bergamot	Labiatae (perennial)	Seeds, root division	Low, about 30 cm (1 ft)	Moist, shady	Replace plants when roots get woody
Borage	Boraginaceae (annual)	Seeds	Medium, up to 70 cm (2 ft 6 in)	Anywhere, even stony ground	Grows to maturity in 5/6 weeks, reseeds itself
Burnet	Rosaceae (perennial)	Seeds, root division	Low, about 30 cm (1 ft)	Chalky	Very hardy, looks after itself. Cut back to produce more leaf growth
Caraway	Umbelliferae (biennial)	Seeds	Medium, up to 60 cm (2 ft)	Anywhere	Prune in the autumn for good second year growth
Chamomile	Compositae (annual)	Seeds	Low, about 30 cm (1 ft)	Anywhere	Sows in rows for easy flower gathering

GARDENER'S CHART *(continued)*

Herb	Family/type	Grow from	Shape and height	Preferred soil	Cultivation
Chervil	Umbelliferae (annual)	Seeds	Medium, up to 60 cm (2 ft)	Moist, half shady	Water regularly in dry spells
Comfrey	Boraginaceae (perennial)	Seeds, root division	Medium, up to 60 cm (2 ft)	Damp, shady	Control self-seeding or it may take over the garden.
Coriander	Umbelliferae (annual)	Seeds	Medium, up to 70 cm (2 ft 6 in)	Light, sunny	If growing for seed leave cut plants on the ground for a few days to complete ripening
Costmary	Compositae (perennial)	Root division	Medium, up to 120 cm (4 ft)	Anywhere dry and sunny	Watch out for roots spreading under more delicate plants
Dandelion	Compositae (perennial)	Seed, root division	Small, up to 20 cm (8 in)	Poor, even stony	Can be treated as weeds and grown in an inconspicuous corner
Dill	Umbelliferae (annual)	Seeds	Medium, up to 70 cm (2 ft 6 in)	Moist, out of the wind	The seedlings are weak so should be weeded carefully
Fennel	Umbelliferae (perennial)	Seeds, root division	Tall, up to 150 cm (5 ft)	Moist, sunny	In autumn cut the plants down to about 10 cm (4 in) to help next year's growth
Fenugreek	Leguminosae (annual)	Seeds	Medium, up to 70 cm (2 ft 6 in)	Well-drained	Allow pods to dry before threshing out the seeds
Horse-radish	Cruciferae (perennial)	Root division	Medium, up to 60 cm (2 ft)	Fairly rich	Keep weed-free to allow roots to develop
Hyssop	Labiatae (perennial)	Seeds, cuttings, root division	Medium, up to 70 cm (2 ft 6 in)	Anywhere	A very hardy plant that needs virtually no care once established

Juniper	Pinaceae (perennial)	Seeds, cuttings	Small tree, up to 4 m (13 ft)	Poor soil is adequate but fertile soil gives greater height	The seeds are very slow to germinate
Lovage	Umbelliferae (perennial)	Seeds, root division	Tall, up to 2·5 m (8 ft)	Moist	Will take about four years to reach full size; allow seeds to develop in darkness
Marjoram	Labiatae (annual and perennial)	Seeds, root division	Low, up to 30 cm (1 ft)	Good, sunny	Water frequently and protect from cold
Mint	Labiatae (perennial)	Root division	Small, up to 25 cm (10 in)	Moist, shady	Restrict the roots or they may damage weaker plants nearby
Oregano	Labiatae (perennial)	Seeds, root division	Medium, up to 70 cm (2 ft 6 in)	Chalky, sunny	Difficult to grow successfully in this country
Parsley	Umbelliferae (biennial)	Seeds	Small, up to 30 cm (1 ft)	Moist, shady	Thin out plants to allow for maximum spread
Purslane	Portulacaceae (annual)	Seeds, cuttings, root division	Small, up to 20 cm (8 in)	Light, sunny	Matures in 6-8 weeks, so can be sown several times each season
Rosemary	Labiatae (perennial)	Cuttings	Tall, up to 2 m (6 ft 6 in)	Sandy, sunny	Protect young plants from frost
Rue	Rutaceae (perennial)	Seeds, cuttings, root division	Medium, up to 60 cm (2 ft)	Poor, sunny	Allow space for the plants to develop sideways
Sage	Labiatae (perennial)	Cuttings	Small, up to 30 cm (1 ft)	Chalky, well-drained	Cut back after flowering to produce next year's growth
Savory	Labiatae (annual-summer savory; perennial-winter savory)	Seeds (summer savory) and cuttings, root division (winter savory)	Small, up to 30 cm (1 ft)	Light, sunny (summer savory), poor (winter savory)	Sow summer variety in late spring to mature with your beans. Winter savory is very hardy

GARDENER'S CHART *(continued)*

Herb	Family/type	Grow from	Shape and height	Preferred soil	Cultivation
Sorrel	Polygonaceae (perennial)	Root division	Medium, up to 60 cm (2 ft)	Light, moist, half-shade	Cut back to prevent plants going to seed and replace when stems become woody
Sweet cicely	Umbelliferae (perennial)	Seeds, root division	Tall, up to 150 cm (5 ft)	Anywhere	
Tarragon	Compositae (perennial)	Cuttings, root division	Medium, up to 1 m (3 ft)	Rich, sunny	Make sure the soil is well-drained and protect from frost
Thyme	Labiatae (perennial)	Seeds, cuttings, root division	Small, 10–20 cm (4–8 in)	Lime or chalky, sunny	Replace plants when they become straggly

Individual pizza ▶

Starters

◀ *Tossed fresh spinach salad; Apple,*
raisin and walnut salad; Italian pepper salad;
Rainbow coleslaw; Minted cucumber and celery

Cheese baked tomatoes with basil

8 large tomatoes, skinned and sliced
75 g (3 oz) Parmesan cheese, freshly
  grated
salt and freshly ground black pepper
5 ml (1 level tsp) dried basil or 15 ml
  (1 tbsp) fresh chopped basil
150 ml (5 fl oz) cream

Serves 4

Arrange the tomato slices in 4 individual
soufflé dishes. Sprinkle with the cheese,
salt and pepper. Dust the tops with the
basil and spoon a little cream over each.
Bake in the oven at 190°C (375°F) mark
5 for about 15 minutes. Serve hot, with
warm bread rolls.

Avocado with herb dressing

5 ml (1 level tsp) dried mixed herbs or
  15 ml (1 tbsp) fresh chopped herbs,
  including chives, basil, tarragon and
  chervil
150 ml (5 fl oz) soured cream
4 drops Tabasco sauce, to taste
salt and pepper
2 avocados
fresh or dried chopped chives for garnish

Serves 4

If you are using dried mixed herbs, stir
them into the soured cream and leave for
30 minutes. Add fresh herbs to the soured
cream just before using. Stir in the
Tabasco sauce and seasoning, then
lightly chill it. Cut the avocados in half
lengthwise, remove the stones and fill
the cavities with the cream mixture.
Serve garnished with chopped chives.

This is delicious alone but, if you
wish, a few peeled prawns, flaked

canned crab meat or tuna can be added
to the cream dressing before filling the
avocados.

*Jellied tomato rings with cottage cheese

450 g (1 lb) ripe tomatoes
15 ml (1 tbsp) onion flakes or 1 medium
  onion, skinned and chopped
1·25 ml ($\frac{1}{4}$ level tsp) minced garlic or 1
  small clove garlic, skinned and chop-
  ped
1 bayleaf
1·25 ml ($\frac{1}{4}$ level tsp) dried tarragon or
  5 ml (1 level tsp) fresh chopped
  tarragon
6 black peppercorns
5 ml (1 level tsp) sugar
2·5 ml ($\frac{1}{2}$ level tsp) salt
pinch celery salt
pinch ground nutmeg
15 ml (1 level tbsp) powdered gelatine
15 ml (1 tbsp) vinegar
45 ml (3 tbsps) lemon juice
150 g (5 oz) cottage cheese
dried or freshly chopped chives

Serves 4–6

Quarter the tomatoes and discard the
pips. Put them in a pan with the onion,
garlic, bayleaf, tarragon, peppercorns,
sugar, salts and nutmeg. Cover and cook
gently until the tomatoes are a pulp
and the onion is tender. Remove the
bayleaf and rub the tomato mixture
through a sieve.

Dissolve the gelatine in 30 ml (2
tbsps) water in a small basin over hot
water. Add the vinegar and lemon juice
to the tomato purée and make it up to
500 ml (1 pt) if necessary with cold water.
Add the gelatine, pour into four or six
individual ring moulds and leave to set.

To serve, turn out the tomato rings
on to small plates and put 15 ml (1 tbsp)

of cottage cheese in the centre of each, then sprinkle with chopped chives.

Prawns in soured cream sauce

10 ml (2 level tsps) dried minced onion or 1 small onion, skinned and finely chopped
25 g (1 oz) butter
5 ml (1 level tsp) curry powder
100 g (4 oz) frozen prawns, thawed
150 ml ($\frac{1}{4}$ pt) soured cream
salt and ground black pepper
sliced cucumber
paprika for garnish

Serves 4

Soak the dried onion in 15 ml (1 tbsp) water for 5 minutes and drain it. Melt the butter and fry the onion until soft but not coloured. Add the curry powder and cook for 1–2 minutes. Add the prawns and sauté for 1–2 minutes, then let the mixture cool.

Add the soured cream, season to taste and chill. Serve on a bed of finely sliced cucumber in individual dishes, sprinkled with paprika.

Mackerel with horse-radish cream

4 small mackerel
salt
fish seasoning
4 small bayleaves
peppercorns
2·5 ml ($\frac{1}{2}$ level tsp) dill seed
60 ml (4 tbsps) double cream, whipped
60 ml (4 tbsps) mayonnaise
5 ml (1 tsp) creamed horseradish
lemon wedges and parsley for garnish

Serves 4

Remove the heads, fins and entrails from the fish, wash them well, sprinkle the cavities with a little salt and fish seasoning and stuff each fish with a bayleaf, 2–3 peppercorns and a pinch of dill seed. Wrap each fish loosely in foil and place in a dish with 2·5 cm (1 in) of water. Cook in the oven at 180°C (350°F) mark 4 for 20 minutes. Leave to cool in the foil. Meanwhile fold the cream, mayonnaise and horseradish together. When the fish is cold remove skin and bones. Place the fillets on individual serving plates and garnish with lemon and parsley. Serve the sauce separately and offer buttered brown bread.

*Cucumber à la grecque

1 large cucumber
63-g (2$\frac{1}{4}$-oz) can tomato paste
300 ml ($\frac{1}{2}$ pt) water
juice of 1 lemon
45 ml (3 tbsps) olive oil
10 ml (2 level tsps) minced onion or 1 small onion, skinned and chopped
pinch of garlic granules or $\frac{1}{2}$ clove garlic, skinned and chopped
pinch of dried parsley or 1 sprig of fresh parsley
pinch of dried thyme or 1 sprig of fresh thyme
pinch of dried fennel seed or 1 sprig of fresh fennel
8 coriander seeds
1 bayleaf
pinch salt
freshly chopped parsley to garnish

Serves 4

Peel the cucumber and cut it in half lengthways. Remove the seeds and cut it into $\frac{1}{2}$-in pieces. Put the remaining ingredients into a saucepan and bring to the boil. Add the cucumber and simmer for 15 minutes. Using a perforated spoon, lift the pieces of cucumber into a dish. Strain the tomato liquor over the cucumber and chill. Serve in individual dishes sprinkled with chopped parsley and accompanied by hot French bread.

Pickled cider herrings

4 medium sized herrings, cleaned and
   boned
salt and freshly ground black pepper
15 ml (1 tbsp) dried onion flakes or 1
   small onion, skinned and sliced
5 ml (1 level tsp) mixed pickling spice
2 bayleaves
pinch dried parsley or a few fresh parsley
   stalks
60 ml (4 tbsps) water
60 ml (4 tbsps) dry cider
60 ml (4 tbsps) malt vinegar
slices of lemon and watercress to garnish

Serves 4

Sprinkle the fish with the salt and pepper and roll up from the head end. Pack them into a fairly shallow ovenproof dish and add the onion, pickling spice, bayleaves and the parsley. Pour in the water, cider and vinegar. Cover with a lid or aluminium foil. Bake in the centre of the oven at 170°C (325°F) mark 3 for about 1 hour, until tender. Leave to cool in the liquor, then chill. Garnish with lemon slices and watercress and serve with crusty brown bread.

Potted shrimps

225 g (8 oz) peeled fresh or frozen
   shrimps
100 g (4 oz) salted butter
2·5 ml ($\frac{1}{2}$ level tsp) ground mace
1·25 ml ($\frac{1}{4}$ level tsp) mixed spice
2·5 ml ($\frac{1}{2}$ level tsp) ground black pepper
2·5 ml ($\frac{1}{2}$ level tsp) paprika
clarified butter

Serves 4

Heat the shrimps very slowly in the

butter, without allowing them to bubble at all. Mix in the spices. Toss over a brisk heat then pour into four small pots or glasses. Leave these to become quite cold and then cover with a little clarified butter. Use within a few days. Serve in pots or turn out on to plates with a crisp lettuce leaf. Serve with lemon wedges and brown bread or melba toast.

*Marinaded mushrooms

450 g (1 lb) small button mushrooms
juice of 1 lemon
2·5 ml ($\frac{1}{2}$ level tsp) salt
150 ml ($\frac{1}{4}$ pt) wine vinegar
60 ml (4 tbsps) olive oil
15 ml (1 level tbsp) dried minced onion
   or 1 medium onion, skinned and
   and chopped
large pinch garlic salt or 1 clove garlic,
   skinned and crushed
pinch dried thyme, or 1 sprig of fresh
   thyme
2·5 ml ($\frac{1}{2}$ level tsp) dried parsley or 2
   sprigs of fresh parsley
1 bayleaf
3 peppercorns
6 coriander seeds
chopped parsley

Serves 4

Wash the mushrooms and put them in a saucepan with the lemon juice, salt and enough cold water to cover. Bring to the boil, cover and simmer gently for 10 minutes. Drain and put them in a deep serving dish.

Put all the remaining ingredients except the chopped parsley in a stainless steel pan. Bring to the boil, simmer for 10 minutes, then cover and leave to stand until cool. Strain the marinade over the mushrooms, cover and leave to stand in a cool place for several hours or overnight. Serve sprinkled with chopped parsley and offer buttered brown bread.

Seafood cocktail

2·5 ml ($\frac{1}{2}$ level tsp) dried dill or fennel, or 7·5 ml (1$\frac{1}{2}$ level tsps) chopped fresh dill or fennel
5 ml (1 level tsp) dried chives, or 15 ml (1 tbsp) chopped fresh chives
15 ml (1 tbsp) lemon juice
42-g (1$\frac{1}{2}$-oz) can dressed crab
175 g (6 oz) cooked white fish, flaked
salt and pepper
$\frac{1}{4}$ cucumber, finely chopped
150 ml ($\frac{1}{4}$ pt) soured cream
sliced lemon for garnish

Serves 4

If you are using dried herbs, mix them with the lemon juice $\frac{1}{2}$ hour before required. Drain the crab meat, flake and mix it with the white fish, then season with the salt and pepper. Arrange the chopped cucumber in the base of four small glasses or dishes. Whip the soured cream with the lemon juice and herbs, add the fish and spoon it on to the cucumber. Garnish with slices of lemon. Serve at once with buttered brown bread.

Kipper pâté

450 g (1 lb) kippers
1 bayleaf
5 ml (1 level tsp) dried thyme or a few sprigs of fresh thyme
75 g (3 oz) butter
juice of $\frac{1}{2}$ a lemon
60 ml (4 tbsps) cream, lightly whipped
freshly ground black pepper
1·25 ml ($\frac{1}{4}$ level tsp) ground mace
lemon wedges and parsley to garnish

Serves 4

Place the fish in a frying pan with the bayleaf and the thyme – add water to cover, bring to the boil, cover and simmer gently for 5 minutes or until the fish is tender. Remove the kippers from the liquid. Discard the skin and the bones. Put the flesh into a bowl and mash it well with a fork, then let it cool. Beat in the butter, lemon juice, cream, pepper and mace. Turn the pâté into a 600-ml (1-pt) serving dish and leave to cool. Garnish with lemon wedges and parsley and serve with freshly made toast.

Liver pâté

300 ml ($\frac{1}{2}$ pt) milk
1 bayleaf
blade of mace
225 g (8 oz) thinly cut streaky bacon rashers, rinded
450 g (1 lb) pig's liver
175 g (6 oz) fat streaky bacon
large pinch of garlic granules or 1 small clove garlic, skinned and crushed
10 ml (2 level tsps) dried minced onion or 1 small onion, skinned and chopped
25 g (1 oz) butter
45 ml (3 level tbsps) plain flour
5 ml (1 level tsp) dried oregano
salt and ground black pepper

Serves 4

Put the milk, bayleaf and mace in a saucepan. Bring to the boil. Remove from the heat, cover and leave to infuse. Using a knife, stretch the bacon rashers and use them to line a loaf tin measuring 19 by 9·5 by 5·5 cm (7$\frac{1}{2}$ by 3$\frac{3}{4}$ by 2$\frac{1}{4}$ in) – top measurements. Wash the liver, remove the rind from the fat bacon, and mince them together. Add the garlic and onion.

Strain the milk. Melt the butter, stir in the flour and cook gently for 2 minutes. Remove the pan from the heat and gradually stir in the seasoned milk. Bring it to the boil, stirring, and cook for 2 minutes. Add the minced liver, bacon and oregano and season generously. Pour into the prepared tin and cover with greaseproof paper and foil. Stand the tin in a roasting tin with 2·5 cm (1 in) water. Cook in the oven at 170°C (325°F) mark 3 for about 2 hours. Cool in the tin. Turn out the pâté and serve garnished with tomato and parsley.

Minestrone milanese

350 g (12 oz) potato, peeled
225 g (8 oz) cabbage heart, shredded
100 g (4 oz) celery, washed
20 ml (1½ level tbsps) dried minced onion or 175 g (6 oz) onion, skinned
3 tomatoes, skinned and quartered
60 ml (4 tbsps) oil
50 g (2 oz) green (unsmoked) streaky bacon, rinded and finely diced
1·7 l (3 pt) white stock
1·25 ml (¼ level tsp) garlic granules or 1 clove garlic, skinned and crushed
100 g (4 oz) ham in 1 piece, diced
2·5 ml (½ level tsp) celery salt
freshly ground black pepper
bouquet garni
50 g (2 oz) frozen peas
40 g (1½ oz) Parmesan cheese, freshly grated
5 ml (1 level tsp) dried parsley or 15 ml (1 tbsp) fresh chopped parsley

Serves 4

Prepare all the vegetables and cut them into small dice. Heat the oil and fry the bacon until cooked but not brown. Add the prepared fresh vegetables and cook for 5 minutes more, stirring frequently. Drain and put them in a large flameproof casserole or saucepan. Pour over the stock, add the dried onion, if you are using this, garlic, ham, seasoning and bouquet garni. Simmer slowly, covered, for 2 hours. Remove bouquet

garni, add the peas, cheese and parsley and cook for a further 10 minutes before serving.

Easy tomato soup

15 ml (1 level tbsp) dried minced onion or 1 medium sized onion, skinned and chopped
3 cloves
992-g (2-lb 3-oz) can tomatoes
pinch of dried or sprig of fresh parsley
1 bayleaf
5 ml (1 level tsp) salt
ground pepper
1·25 ml (¼ level tsp) freshly grated nutmeg
50 g (2 oz) butter
45 ml (3 level tbsps) flour
450 ml (¾ pt) milk
150 ml (¼ pt) light stock
30–45 ml (2–3 tbsps) single cream

Serves 4

Put the onions, cloves, tomatoes with their juice, parsley, bayleaf, seasoning and nutmeg in a saucepan. Bring them to the boil, reduce the heat, cover and simmer for 1 hour. Melt the butter in another pan and blend in the flour to give a smooth paste. Cook the roux for 2–3 minutes before gradually stirring in the milk. Bring the sauce to the boil, stirring, reduce the heat and simmer for 5 minutes.

Remove the bayleaf and cloves from the tomato mixture. Purée it in an electric blender and pass it through a fine sieve to remove the pips. Add it to the white sauce and mix them well together, or combine them in the blender. Stir in the stock and cream, check seasoning and reheat the soup to serving temperature but do not boil. Just before serving, whirl some more cream over the surface.

Chervil soup

75 g (3 oz) butter or margarine
2 leeks, washed and chopped
15 ml (1 level tbsp) dried minced onion
  or 1 medium onion, skinned and
  chopped
2 large potatoes, peeled and chopped
1·1 l (2 pt) boiling stock or water
salt and pepper
10 ml (2 level tsps) dried chervil or 30 ml
  (2 tbsps) chopped fresh chervil

Serves 4

Melt 50 g (2 oz) fat in a saucepan and
gently fry the fresh vegetables, stirring
until transparent. Add the liquid, with
the dried onion, seasoning to taste and
and the dried chervil if used. Bring the
soup to the boil and simmer slowly for
at least $\frac{1}{2}$ hour. Sieve the vegetables,
return them to the pan and boil for 5
minutes; then add the fresh chervil and
a knob of butter.

* Gazpacho

15 ml (1 level tbsp) sweet pepper flakes
  or $\frac{1}{2}$ sweet red pepper, seeded and
  chopped
100 g (4 oz) green pepper, seeded and
  chopped
1 medium cucumber, roughly chopped
450 g (1 lb) fully ripened tomatoes,
  roughly chopped
50–100 g (2–4 oz) onion, skinned and
  chopped
1·25 ml ($\frac{1}{4}$ level tsp) garlic salt or
  1 clove garlic, skinned and crushed
45 ml (3 tbsps) oil
45 ml (3 tbsps) wine vinegar
425-g (15-oz) can tomato juice
30 ml (2 level tbsps) tomato paste
1·25 ml ($\frac{1}{4}$ level tsp) salt
croûtons

Serves 4

If using pepper flakes, pour over 60 ml
(4 tbsps) boiling water, leave for 10
minutes, then drain. Reserve a little
green pepper and the croûtons, then
mix all the ingredients together in a
basin. Purée them in an electric blender
a little at a time, return the purée to the
bowl and add a few ice cubes. Serve the
soup garnished with very finely diced
green pepper and croûtons.

Chicken and tarragon soup

1 chicken carcass
15 ml (1 level tbsp) dried minced onion
  or 1 medium onion, skinned and
  chopped
1 bayleaf
1 blade of mace
4 peppercorns
5 ml (1 level tsp) salt
900 ml ($1\frac{1}{2}$ pt) water
1 stick of celery, finely chopped
1 small carrot, pared and finely chopped
30 ml (2 level tbsps) cornflour
300 ml ($\frac{1}{2}$ pt) milk
2·5 ml ($\frac{1}{2}$ level tsp) dried tarragon or 6
  fresh sprigs of tarragon, chopped
100 g (4 oz) cooked chicken meat, chopped
2·5 ml ($\frac{1}{2}$ level tsp) chicken seasoning
blanched toasted almonds for garnish

Serves 4

Break up the carcass and put it in a pan
with the onion, bayleaf, mace, peppercorns, salt and water. Bring to the boil,
cover and simmer for 45 minutes. Strain.
Return the stock to the saucepan with the
celery and carrot. Blend the cornflour
to a smooth paste with the milk, stir it
into the pan and bring to the boil,
stirring. Add the tarragon and chicken.
Add the chicken seasoning and simmer,

covered, for 30 minutes. Adjust the seasoning and serve sprinkled with blanched toasted almonds.

Iced cucumber and chive or mint soup

10 ml (2 level tsps) dried mint or chives, or 30 ml (2 tbsps) fresh chopped mint or chives
1 large unpeeled cucumber
300 ml ($\frac{1}{2}$ pt) yoghurt
1·25 ml ($\frac{1}{4}$ level tsp) garlic salt or 1 clove garlic, skinned and chopped, optional
30 ml (2 tbsps) wine vinegar
salt and pepper
300 ml ($\frac{1}{2}$ pt) ice cold milk

Serves 4

If you are using dried herbs mix them with 10 ml (2 tsps) boiling water and leave for 5 minutes.

Grate the cucumber into a bowl. Stir in the yoghurt, garlic (if used), vinegar and mint or chives. Season to taste and chill. Just before serving stir in the milk. Spoon into bowls and serve.

Parsley soup

30 ml (2 level tbsps) dried parsley or 50 g (2 oz) bunch of fresh parsley
25 g (1 oz) butter
25 ml (1$\frac{1}{2}$ level tbsps) dried minced onion or 1$\frac{1}{2}$ medium onions, skinned and finely chopped
350 g (12 oz) old potatoes, peeled and diced
900 ml (1$\frac{1}{2}$ pt) chicken stock
30 ml (2 tbsps) creamy milk
salt and white pepper

Serves 4

If you are using fresh parsley, remove the tops, leave the stalks whole and chop the leaves finely. Melt the butter in a saucepan, add the fresh onion and potato and cook gently for 5 minutes until softened. Add the dried onion (if used), stock and parsley stalks and cook for 10 minutes until the potato is soft. Remove the parsley stalks and blend or pass the soup through a sieve. Return it to the saucepan, add the fresh or dried parsley and simmer gently for 5 minutes. Stir in the milk. Adjust the seasoning.

Cream of fish soup

225 g (8 oz) cod fillet or any white fish
900 ml (1$\frac{1}{2}$ pt) cold water
salt and freshly ground black pepper
50 g (2 oz) butter
45 ml (3 level tbsps) flour
300 ml ($\frac{1}{2}$ pt) creamy milk
10 ml (2 level tsps) dried dill weed or fennel or 30 ml (2 tbsps) chopped fresh dill or fennel
1 large potato, peeled, diced and cooked
10 ml (2 tsps) lemon juice
fish seasoning

Serves 4

Wipe the fish and put it in a large saucepan. Pour the cold water over, season and bring almost to the boil. Off the heat, skim off the surface froth. Carefully lift the fish, using a draining spoon, on to a plate. Remove and discard the skin and bones and flake the fish into bite-size portions – leave these to one side. Strain and reserve the stock.

Melt the butter in a large saucepan, stir in the flour and cook gently for 2 minutes. Remove the pan from the heat and gradually stir in the fish stock and milk. Stir in the herbs. Bring the sauce to the boil, stirring, and cook for 2 minutes. Reduce the heat to simmering point, add the potatoes, fish and lemon juice. Season to taste with fish seasoning, salt and pepper. Simmer gently for 5 minutes. Serve with warm French bread.

*Mint dressed grapefruit

5 ml (1 level tsp) dried or 15 ml (1 tbsp) chopped fresh mint
2 large grapefruits
100 g (4 oz) white grapes
20 ml (4 tsps) lemon juice
10 ml (2 level tsps) caster sugar
15 ml (1 tbsp) olive oil
salt and freshly ground pepper

Serves 4

If you are using dried mint, mix it with 5 ml (1 tsp) boiling water and leave for 5 minutes. Halve the grapefruits and cut round each half, loosening the flesh from the outer skin. Cut between the segments to loosen the flesh from the membrane. Peel and pip the grapes. Whisk the remaining ingredients together with the mint, add the grapes and place a spoonful in the centre of each grapefruit.

Spiced hot grapefruit

2 large grapefruits
30 ml (2 tbsps) dry sherry, optional
30 ml (2 level tbsps) caster sugar
10 ml (2 level tsps) ground cinnamon
large knob of butter

Serves 4

Prepare grapefruits as for mint dressed grapefruit. Add 7·5 ml ($\frac{1}{2}$ tbsp) sherry to

each half, if you wish. Mix the sugar and cinnamon together and sprinkle over the grapefruit. Dot with the butter and grill lightly under a medium heat until the sugar has melted and the grapefruit is heated through.

Hot Caribbean grapefruit

2 large grapefruits
60 ml (4 level tbsps) brown sugar
2.5 ml ($\frac{1}{2}$ level tsp) ground ginger
large knob of butter

Serves 4

Prepare the grapefruits and grill as for spiced hot grapefruit.

*Melon and ginger cocktail

30 ml (2 level tbsps) caster sugar
5 ml (1 level tsp) ground ginger
60 ml (4 tbsps) water
1 small ripe melon
1 large grapefruit
1 large orange

Serves 4

Put the sugar, ginger and the water in a very small pan, stir and dissolve over a low heat. Boil for 1 minute, then leave to cool.

Cut the top off the melon, remove the seeds and scoop out the flesh. Cut it into cubes and chill the empty melon shell. Remove the skin and pith from the grapefruit and orange and cut out the segments. Mix the segments together with the melon cubes, ginger syrup and juices. Return the mixture to the chilled shell of the melon or serve in glasses.

Tuna stuffed eggs

6 large eggs
99-g (3½-oz) can tuna fish
60 ml (4 level tbsps) thick mayonnaise
15 ml (1 tbsp) lemon juice
1·25 ml (¼ level tsp) dried tarragon or
   few sprigs fresh tarragon, chopped
salt and ground black pepper
4 large tomatoes, sliced
French dressing
15 ml (1 tbsp) chopped fresh parsley

Serves 4–6

Place the eggs in a saucepan, cover with cold water and bring to the boil; reduce the heat and simmer for 10 minutes. Run the eggs under cold water. Drain the fish and mash it with a fork. Shell and halve the eggs lengthways, then remove the yolks and add to the tuna with the mayonnaise, lemon juice, tarragon, salt and pepper to taste. Pile the the mixture back into the whites and arrange them on tomato slices dressed with French dressing. Sprinkle over the chopped parsley.

* Cheese baked eggs

4 large eggs
60 ml (4 tbsps) double cream
50 g (2 oz) Cheddar cheese, grated
15 ml (1 tbsp) lemon juice
15 ml (1 tbsp) dry white wine or cider
5 ml (1 level tsp) dry mustard
1·25 ml (¼ level tsp) salt
pinch ground black pepper
2·5 ml (½ level tsp) dried basil
25 g (1 oz) fresh white breadcrumbs

Serves 4

Break the eggs into individual buttered ramekins. Mix together the cream, cheese, lemon juice, wine (or cider), mustard, salt and the pepper. Cover the eggs with the seasoned cream and sprinkle with the breadcrumbs mixed with basil. Place dishes in a roasting tin with hot water to come halfway up, and bake in the oven at 190°C (375°F) mark 5 for 15–20 minutes. Serve immediately.

* Cottage cheese and ham cocottes

25 g (1 oz) butter, melted
225 g (8 oz) cottage cheese
2 eggs
1 slice cooked ham, chopped
100 g (4 oz) button mushrooms, wiped
5 ml (1 level tsp) minced onion or 1 small
   onion, finely chopped and softened
   in a little butter
sea salt and pepper
5 ml (1 level tsp) dried herbs or 15 ml
   (1 tbsp) fresh chopped herbs, either
   parsley, chervil or tarragon
paprika

Serves 4

Brush four individual ovenproof dishes with melted butter. Place them on a baking sheet. Beat the cottage cheese and eggs together. Stir in the ham, mushrooms and onion, then season to taste and mix in the herbs. Divide the mixture between the four dishes and cook in the oven at 200°C (400°F) mark 6 for 10–15 minutes. Serve sprinkled with a little paprika.

Everyday Dinners

Chili con carne

15 ml (1 tbsp) corn oil
700 g (1½ lb) minced lean beef
175 g (6 oz) onion, skinned and chopped
15 ml (1 level tbsp) flour
30 ml (2 level tbsps) tomato paste
10 ml (2 level tsps) chili seasoning
1·25 ml (¼ level tsp) garlic granules
1·25 ml (¼ level tsp) cayenne pepper
5 ml (1 level tsp) dried sweet pepper
    flakes
396-g (14-oz) can tomatoes
salt
freshly ground black pepper
425-g (15-oz) can red kidney beans,
    drained

Serves 6

Heat the oil in a large saucepan and quickly brown the beef Add the onion and cook a little longer. Sprinkle the flour over and mix it well with the meat, add the tomato paste, chili seasoning, garlic granules, cayenne, pepper flakes and tomatoes with their juice. Season with salt and black pepper and mix well. Bring to the boil, reduce the heat, cover and simmer for 40 minutes. Add the kidney beans after 30 minutes. Serve with boiled rice.

* Spiced silverside

1·8 kg (4 lb) piece of salted silverside
15 ml (1 tbsp) dried onion flakes or 1
    medium onion, skinned and sliced
2 carrots, pared and sliced
1 small turnip, peeled and sliced
1–2 sticks of celery, chopped
8 cloves
100 g (4 oz) soft brown sugar
2·5 ml (½ level tsp) dry mustard
5 ml (1 level tsp) ground cinnamon
juice of 1 orange

Serves 8

Soak the meat for several hours or overnight, then rinse it, put in a large pan with the vegetables, cover with water and bring slowly to the boil. Remove any scum, cover with a lid and simmer until tender, allowing 3–3½ hours. Allow it to cool in the liquid.

Drain the meat, put it into a roasting tin and stick the cloves into the fat. Mix together the remaining ingredients and spread over the meat. Bake in the oven at 180°C (350°F) mark 4 for ¾–1 hour, basting from time to time. Serve hot or cold. If you wish, you can press the meat after cooking; fit it snugly into a casserole or foil-lined tin, spoon a little of the liquor over and place a small plate on top, with a heavy weight. Leave in a cold place.

Beef olives

8 thin slices of topside
seasoned flour
40 g (1½ oz) fat
30 ml (2 tbsps) dried onion flakes or 2
    medium onions, skinned and chopped
100 g (4 oz) mushrooms, wiped and
    finely chopped
400 ml (¾ pt) beef stock or water
salt and pepper

For the stuffing
100 g (4 oz) fresh white breadcrumbs
50 g (2 oz) shredded suet
grated rind of ½ lemon
20 ml (4 level tsps) dried or 60 ml (4
    tbsps) chopped fresh parsley
5 ml (1 level tsp) each of dried marjoram
    and thyme, or 15 ml (1 tbsp) chopped
    fresh marjoram and thyme
pinch of grated nutmeg
salt and pepper
beaten egg to mix

Serves 4

Combine the ingredients for the stuffing and bind with the beaten egg. Spread each slice of meat with stuffing, roll them up and secure with fine string; toss in seasoned flour. Heat the fat in a pan, sauté the fresh onion and mushrooms until the onion is transparent then, using a draining spoon, transfer them to a casserole. Reheat the pan juice and brown the beef olives lightly in it, then transfer them to the casserole with the mushrooms and onions. If you are using dried onions, add them at this stage. Add 30 ml (2 level tbsps) seasoned flour to the pan, brown it well and gradually stir in the stock or water. Bring to the boil and season to taste with salt and pepper. Pour the sauce over the olives. Cover and cook in the oven at 180°C (350°F) mark 4 for 1½ hours. Remove the string before serving the olives.

Goulash

25 g (1 oz) dripping or lard
1 large onion, skinned and sliced
550 g (1¼ lb) chuck steak, cut into cubes
15 ml (1 level tbsp) paprika
60 ml (4 level tbsps) flour
10 ml (2 level tsps) salt
1·25 ml (¼ level tsp) ground pepper
15 ml (1 level tbsp) tomato paste
300 ml (½ pt) beef or bone stock
396-g (14-oz) can tomatoes
1 large green pepper, seeded and sliced
5 ml (1 level tsp) caster sugar
1 bayleaf
1·25 ml (¼ level tsp) grated nutmeg
soured cream
chopped fresh parsley to garnish

Serves 4

Melt the fat in a flameproof casserole and fry the onion, cubed steak and paprika for about 5 minutes, turning frequently until the meat is sealed and brown. Re-

move the casserole from the heat and stir in the flour, salt, pepper and tomato paste. Stir in the stock and tomatoes with their juice and heat gently, stirring until the sauce thickens. Add the sliced pepper, sugar, bayleaf and nutmeg. Simmer gently, covered, for about 1½ hours or until the meat is tender. Remove the bayleaf. To serve, spoon the soured cream over the top and sprinkle with chopped parsley.

Crisp top casseroled beef

30 ml (2 tbsps) cooking oil
700 g (1½ lb) stewing steak, cut into small pieces
15 ml (1 tbsp) dried onion flakes or 1 medium onion, skinned and chopped
225 g (8 oz) carrot, pared and thinly sliced
184-g (6½-oz) can tomatoes
30 ml (2 level tbsps) flour
300 ml (½ pt) beef stock
5 ml (1 level tsp) dried basil, or 15 ml (1 tbsp) chopped fresh basil
1 bouquet garni
salt and freshly ground black pepper
small pkt plain potato crisps
50 g (2 oz) Cheddar cheese, grated
fresh parsley for garnish, optional

Serves 4

Heat the oil in a flameproof casserole, add the meat and quickly seal the surfaces. Remove the beef from the oil. If using fresh onion, add it with the carrot to the reheated oil and cook them for 2–3 minutes. Return the meat to the casserole with the tomatoes and their juice. Cream the flour with a little stock, stir in the rest of the stock and the dried onion if used. Pour the mixture over the beef and vegetables, add the herbs, salt and pepper and bring to the boil, stirring. Cover and put the casserole in the oven at 170°C (325°F) mark 3 about 1½ hours.

Drain the meat well leaving the juices in the casserole. Put the meat in a deep ovenproof dish and keep it warm. Reduce the juices by half by boiling rapidly, then pour over and fork through the meat. Arrange crisps and cheese alternately over the beef to cover it. Return the dish to the oven at 190°C (375°F) mark 5 for 5–10 minutes to melt the cheese. Garnish with parsley, if you wish.

Steak and mushroom pie

30 ml (2 tbsps) dried onion flakes or 1 large onion, skinned and chopped
700 g (1½ lb) stewing steak
30 ml (2 level tbsps) flour
5 ml (1 level tsp) salt
freshly ground black pepper
30 ml (2 tbsps) cooking oil
300 ml (½ pt) beef stock
100 g (4 oz) mushrooms, wiped and sliced
1 bayleaf
large pinch of dried parsley or 5 ml (1 tsp) chopped fresh parsley
pinch each of ground cloves and dried or fresh marjoram
5 ml (1 tsp) Worcestershire sauce

For the pastry
200 g (7 oz) plain flour
5 ml (1 level tsp) mixed dried herbs
salt
100 g (3½ oz) fat (half lard, half butter or margarine)
cold water to mix
beaten egg to glaze

Serves 4–5

If you are using dried onion, soak it in warm water for 10 minutes, then drain it and set aside. Wipe the meat, cut it into small even size pieces. Mix the flour

the salt and 1·25 ml (¼ level tsp) pepper. Toss the meat in the seasoned flour.

Heat the oil in a pan, add the onion (fresh or dried) and fry gently until golden. Add the meat and brown it on all sides. Gradually stir in the stock, then add the mushrooms, bayleaf, parsley, cloves, marjoram and Worcestershire sauce. Adjust the seasoning to taste, then cover and simmer gently on top of the stove for 1½ hours or until the meat is tender, then let it cool.

Meanwhile make the pastry. Put the flour, herbs and a large pinch of salt in a bowl. Rub in the fats and add enough water to make a stiff dough. Put the cooked meat into a 1·1-l (2-pt) pie dish, with enough gravy to half fill it. Roll out the pastry 2·5 cm (1 in) larger than the top of the dish. Cut off a 1-cm (½-in) strip from round the edge of the pastry and put this strip round the dampened rim of the dish. Damp the pastry edge with water and put the lid on top of the pie, trimming and flaking the edges. Decorate, if you wish, with leaves made from the pastry trimmings. Brush with beaten egg to glaze and bake in the oven at 220°C (425°F) mark 7 for 20 minutes. Reduce the heat to 180°C (350°F) mark 4 and cook for a further 20 minutes.

Roast loin of pork

2 kg (4½ lb) rib-end loin of pork, chined
1·25 ml (¼ level tsp) each of dried sage, *fines herbes*, dried thyme and dried rosemary
1·25 ml (¼ level tsp) garlic salt
freshly ground black pepper
cooking oil
salt

Serves 8

Ask the butcher to score the rind evenly and deeply, and to leave the rib bones protruding about 2·5 cm (1 in). Use scissors to snip between the protruding bones and scrape away the flesh. Mix the herbs and seasoning. Make a shallow pocket between the flesh and fat along the length of the rib bones and press in the seasoning. Tie the joint into a neat shape, especially the kidney end, and rub the rind with oil and salt.

Put the joint either in roaster bags (one on either end, slightly overlapping) or use roasting film. Put it in a baking tin and roast at 190°C (375°F) mark 5 for 25 minutes per 450 g (1 lb) plus 25 minutes extra; 15 minutes before the end of cooking time, remove the roaster bags or film, drain off the juices and return the joint to the tin. Increase the oven temperature to 220°C (425°F) mark 7 to give a really crunchy crackling.

To serve, remove the string and cover bone ends with cutlet frills. Serve with roast potatoes and green vegetables.

* Pork with herbs in cider

4 neck pork chops
salt and ground black pepper
20 ml (1½ tbsps) oil
25 g (1 oz) butter
2·5 ml (½ level tsp) dried basil
2·5 ml (½ level tsp) dried thyme or 7·5 ml (1½ tsps) chopped fresh thyme
2·5 ml (½ level tsp) dried marjoram or 7·5 ml (1½ tsps) chopped fresh marjoram
1 large onion, skinned and chopped
2 large eating apples, peeled, cored and chopped
150 ml (¼ pt) dry cider

Serves 4

Trim any excess fat from the chops and season them well with salt and pepper. Heat the oil and butter in a pan and fry the chops on both sides until golden.

Drain them well, pat off the excess fat with kitchen paper and place them in an ovenproof dish. Sprinkle with the herbs. Fry the onion in the remaining fat until transparent, remove it from the pan, drain well and mix with the apple. Spoon the mixture on to the chops and pour in the cider. Cover and bake in the oven at 180°C (350°F) mark 4 for about 45 minutes. Remove the lid and bake for a further 15 minutes.

* Barbecued spare ribs

4 large pork spare ribs, English cut (700–900 g, 1½–2 lb)
30 ml (2 tbsps) cooking oil
30 ml (2 tbsps) soy sauce
30 ml (2 level tbsps) tomato paste
30 ml (2 tbsps) vinegar
30 ml (2 tbsps) orange juice
60 ml (4 tbsps) water
15 ml (1 level tbsp) brown sugar
2·5 ml (½ level tsp) dry mustard
small pinch ground cloves
1·25 ml (¼ level tsp) coriander seeds
pinch garlic granules or 1 small clove garlic, skinned and chopped
salt and pepper
1 medium onion, skinned and chopped
barbecue seasoning

Serves 4

Remove any excess fat from the meat and place the meat in a shallow dish. Mix together 15 ml (1 tbsp) oil, the soy sauce, tomato paste, vinegar, orange juice, water, sugar, mustard, cloves, coriander, garlic, salt and pepper. Pour this sauce over the pork, cover and leave to marinade for at least 2 hours or overnight if possible.

Remove the meat from the marinade and pat it dry with kitchen paper. Heat the remaining oil in a pan, fry the onion until soft, then remove it from the pan and set aside. Sprinkle the meat with barbecue seasoning and fry in the pan until golden on both sides. Place it in an ovenproof dish, add the onion and pour over the marinade; cover and cook in the oven at 190°C (375°F) mark 5 for $\frac{3}{4}$ hour. Remove the lid and cook for a further 15 minutes, basting occasionally. Remove any excess fat from the sauce and serve it poured over the pork.

Pork and pineapple casserole

700 g (1½ lb) spare rib of pork
50 g (2 oz) butter
15 ml (1 tbsp) dried onion flakes or 1 medium onion, skinned and chopped
30 ml (2 level tbsps) flour
226-g (8-oz) can pineapple slices
200 ml (7 fl oz) water
30 ml (2 level tbsps) tomato paste
1 stick celery, trimmed and chopped
2·5 ml (½ level tsp) dried thyme or 7·5 ml (1½ tsps) chopped fresh thyme
5 ml (1 tsp) dried parsley or 15 ml (1 tbsp) chopped fresh parsley
garlic salt
salt and pepper
1 bayleaf

Serves 4

Remove excess fat from the pork and cut the meat into cubes. Heat the butter in a pan and fry the meat on all sides until golden. Remove the meat from the pan, drain and place it in a casserole dish. If you are using fresh onion, add it to the fat remaining in the pan, fry it until soft, then drain and add it to the pork.

Drain off all but 15 ml (1 tbsp) of the fat in the pan. Stir in the flour and cook gently for 1 minute. Drain the pineapple, cut the fruit into cubes and stir the syrup gradually into the pan, with the water and and tomato paste. Bring the sauce to

the boil, still stirring. If you are using dried onion flakes add them to the sauce at this stage with the celery, pineapple, herbs, garlic salt, salt and pepper to taste. Pour it over the meat, add a bay-leaf, cover and cook in the oven at 170°C (325°F) mark 3 for 1½ hours.

Crumb topped pork chops

4 lean pork chops
50 g (2 oz) fresh white breadcrumbs
5 ml (1 tsp) dried parsley or 15 ml (1 tbsp) fresh chopped parsley
2·5 ml (½ tsp) dried mint or 7·5 ml (1½ tsps) chopped fresh mint
pinch dried thyme
grated rind of 1 lemon
2·5 ml (½ level tsp) coriander seeds, crushed
salt and freshly ground black pepper
1 small egg, beaten

Serves 4

Remove the rind from the chops and put them in a baking tin. Mix the remaining ingredients together and spread them over the chops. Bake in the oven at 200°C (400°F) mark 6 for about 45–50 minutes, or until golden.

Danish meat balls

5 ml (1 level tsp) dried onion flakes, or 1 small onion, skinned and grated
30 ml (2 level tbsps) flour
2·5 ml (½ level tsp) salt
2·5 ml (½ level tsp) ground allspice
1·25 ml (¼ level tsp) ground white pepper
450 g (1 lb) lean pork, finely minced
1 small egg, beaten
60 ml (4 tbsps) milk
50 g (2 oz) butter
30 ml (2 tbsps) oil

Serves 4

If you are using dried onion, soak it in warm water for 10 minutes, then drain. Sift the flour, salt and spices together. Mix with the meat, add the onion (fresh or dried) and egg and enough milk to give a mixture that is soft but will hold its shape. Mix well. Shape the mixture into about 20 small oval balls. Heat the butter and oil and cook the meatballs slowly until brown on all sides (about 8 minutes each side). Drain on kitchen paper and serve with mashed potato and creamed spinach.

Rum basted bacon

15 ml (1 tbsp) soy sauce
2·5 ml ($\frac{1}{2}$ level tsp) dry mustard
15 ml (1 level tbsp) golden syrup
2·5 ml ($\frac{1}{2}$ level tsp) ground ginger
90 ml (6 tbsps) orange juice
30 ml (2 tbsps) rum
garlic salt
ground black pepper
15 ml (1 level tbsp) cornflour
15 ml (1 tbsp) lemon juice
4 bacon chops or gammon steaks

Serves 4

In a small saucepan combine the first eight ingredients. Blend the cornflour with the lemon juice, add a little of the mixture from the saucepan and then return it to the bulk. Bring to the boil, stirring all the time, until the glaze has thickened. Remove from the heat. Cut most of the fat from the bacon chops or gammon steaks and then brush on the glaze. Grill under a moderate heat for 15 minutes. The glaze should be browned and bubbling. Turn several times during cooking to ensure that the meat is cooked right through.

* Tangy chops

50 g (2 oz) butter
4 lamb chops
salt and pepper
10 ml (2 tbsps) lemon juice
5 ml (1 level tsp) dry mustard
10 ml (2 level tsps) dried parsley or
    30 ml (2 tbsps) fresh chopped parsley
2·5 ml ($\frac{1}{2}$ level tsp) dried basil

Serves 4

Melt the butter and fry the chops until brown. Season them with salt and pepper. Mix the remaining ingredients, spoon the mixture over the chops, cover tightly and simmer gently for 30 minutes.

* Grilled lamb chops

4 lamb chops
salt and pepper

Serves 4

Place the chops on an oiled or greased rack 5 cm (2 in) from the preheated grill. Grill for 1 minute on either side to seal the chops, then continue for about 5 minutes on either side. Season with salt and pepper.

* Rosemary or oregano lamb chops

4 lamb chops
10 ml (2 tbsps) lemon juice
5 ml (1 level tsp) dried rosemary or oregano

Serves 4

Sprinkle each chop with lemon juice and herbs, and grill as in previous recipe.

* Barbecued lamb chops

4–6 middle loin chops
barbecue seasoning
1 lemon, sliced
1 medium onion, skinned and chopped
60 ml (4 tbsps) vinegar
5 ml (1 level tsp) salt
5 ml (1 level tsp) chili seasoning
5 ml (1 level tsp) celery seed
60 ml (4 tbsps) Worcestershire sauce
160-g ($5\frac{1}{2}$-oz) can tomato juice
150 ml ($\frac{1}{4}$ pt) water
few drops Tabasco sauce

Serves 3–4

Arrange the chops in a shallow baking dish and sprinkle with barbecue seasoning. On each chop put a slice of lemon and a little chopped onion. Mix all the remaining ingredients together and add to the chops. Bake in the oven at 180°C (350°F) mark 4, for 30–45 minutes, basting the chops frequently with the sauce.

Boiled lamb with dill sauce

900 g (2 lb) best end of neck of lamb, chined
15 ml (1 level tbsp) salt
3–4 peppercorns
1 bayleaf
pinch of dill seeds
chopped fresh dill for garnish

For dill sauce
40 g ($1\frac{1}{2}$ oz) butter
40 g ($1\frac{1}{2}$ oz) flour
400 ml ($\frac{3}{4}$ pt) stock
7·5 ml ($1\frac{1}{2}$ level tsps) dried dill weed or 20 ml ($1\frac{1}{2}$ tbsps) chopped fresh dill
20 ml ($1\frac{1}{2}$ tbsps) vinegar
7·5 ml ($1\frac{1}{2}$ level tsps) sugar
1 egg yolk
salt and pepper

Serves 4

Put the meat in a saucepan and cover with water. Add the salt, peppercorns, bayleaf and dill seeds. Simmer for 1–$1\frac{1}{2}$ hours or until tender. Meanwhile, make the dill sauce – make a roux with the butter and flour, gradually add the stock and simmer for 2–3 minutes, stirring all the time. Add the dill, vinegar and sugar. Remove from the heat and stir in the egg yolk and seasoning.

Remove the meat from the pan, carve into 'chops' and place on a hot dish, sprinkled with a little extra chopped dill. Serve with the dill sauce.

Mint lamb casserole

8 best end of neck cutlets
lamb seasoning
25 g (1 oz) lard
15 ml (1 tbsp) dried onion flakes, or 1 medium onion, skinned and chopped
425-g (15-oz) can peeled tomatoes
pinch of garlic salt
2·5 ml ($\frac{1}{2}$ level tsp) salt
large pinch of ground white pepper
5 ml (1 level tsp) sugar
5 ml (1 level tsp) dried mint or 15 ml (1 tbsp) chopped fresh mint
pinch of ground bayleaves
15 ml (1 tbsp) dried sweet pepper flakes
50 g (2 oz) grated cheese
50 g (2 oz) fresh white breadcrumbs

Serves 4

Trim the excess fat from the cutlets and remove the bone. Sprinkle both sides of the meat with lamb seasoning. Heat the lard in a pan and brown the cutlets on both sides. Remove them from the pan, wipe off excess fat with kitchen paper and place them in a casserole. Add the fresh onion to the pan and fry gently for 3 minutes. Drain and add to the casserole. Mix the tomatoes with their juices, the seasonings, sugar, herbs, sweet pepper flakes and dried onion (if used). Pour over the meat. Cover and cook the casserole in the oven at 170°C (325°F) mark 3 for 1 hour. Remove the lid and sprinkle over the cheese and breadcrumbs mixed together, and bake uncovered for a further 30 minutes.

Veal casserole with thyme

700 g (1½ lb) pie veal
15 ml (1 tbsp) cooking oil
25 g (1 oz) butter
15 ml (1 tbsp) dried onion flakes or 1 onion, skinned and chopped
1 carrot, pared and sliced
100 g (4 oz) mushrooms, wiped and sliced
30 ml (2 level tbsps) flour
300 ml (½ pt) veal or chicken stock (or half stock and half dry white wine or cider)
2·5 ml (½ level tsp) dried thyme or 7·5 ml (1½ tsps) chopped fresh thyme
salt and pepper
freshly chopped parsley for garnish

Serves 4

Cut the meat into cubes, heat the oil and butter in a pan and fry the meat lightly. Lift it out, drain the meat well and place it in a 1·7-l (3-pt) casserole. Fry the fresh onion and carrot in the remaining fat until the onion is transparent, then add them to the veal with the mushrooms.

Add the flour to the fat remaining in the pan and cook gently for 2 minutes. Remove the pan from the heat then gradually stir in the liquid. Bring to the boil, stirring, add the herbs, seasonings and dried onion if you are using it; pour the sauce over the meat. Cover and cook

in the oven at 170°C (325°F) mark 3 for about 1½ hours. Sprinkle with parsley and serve with buttered noodles.

Golden baked chicken joints

10 ml (2 level tsps) dried minced onion
4 chicken portions
chicken seasoning
50 g (2 oz) fresh white breadcrumbs
5 ml (1 level tsp) mixed herbs or dried parsley or 15 ml (1 tbsp) chopped fresh parsley
50 g (2 oz) butter, melted

Serves 4

Soak the minced onion in warm water for 10 minutes, then drain. Wipe the chicken portions and sprinkle them with chicken seasoning. Mix the breadcrumbs with the onion and herbs.

Brush the chicken joints with butter to coat completely, toss them in the herb breadcrumbs and place in a buttered ovenproof dish. Cook them in the oven at 190°C (375°F) mark 5, for about 1 hour or until golden. Baste occasionally during cooking.

* Italian chicken casserole

4 chicken portions
flour
30 ml (2 tbsps) oil
25 g (1 oz) butter
1 green pepper, seeded and chopped
30 ml (2 tbsps) dried onion flakes, or 1 large onion, skinned and sliced
chicken seasoning
425-g (15-oz) can tomatoes
5 ml (1 level tsp) Italian seasoning
pinch garlic salt

Serves 4

Wipe the chicken portions and toss them in flour. Heat the oil and butter in a pan. Lightly fry the pepper and fresh onion until the onion is transparent, remove from the pan with a draining spoon and drain on kitchen paper. Reheat the pan fat and fry the chicken portions until golden. Drain well, sprinkle with chicken seasoning and place in a casserole with the onion (fresh or dried) and pepper. Mix the tomatoes and juice with the seasoning and pour them over the chicken. Cover and cook in the oven at 170°C (325°F) mark 3 for 1½ hours. Serve with fresh green vegetables and jacket potatoes.

* French-style roast chicken

1–1·4-kg (2¼–3-lb) oven ready chicken
5 ml (1 level tsp) dried tarragon or parsley or 5–6 sprigs fresh tarragon or parsley
large knob of butter
pepper and salt
2 rashers of bacon
150 ml (¼ pt) chicken stock
150 ml (¼ pt) dry white wine
25g (1 oz) flour
watercress to garnish

Serves 3–4

Wipe the inside of the chicken, then put the tarragon or parsley inside it, with the butter and some pepper. Cover the breast of the bird with rashers of bacon, place it in a roasting tin, add the stock and wine and roast in the oven at 190°C (375°F) mark 5 for 45–50 minutes, basting every 15 minutes with the stock. Remove the bacon during the last 15 minutes to let the breast brown. Place the chicken on a serving dish and keep it warm. In a saucepan, blend the flour to a smooth cream with a little water and slowly add the chicken juices. Bring the sauce to the boil, simmer for 2–3 minutes, stirring, adjust the seasoning and serve separately. Garnish the chicken with watercress.

Casserole of ox heart

1 ox heart
30 ml (2 level tbsps) seasoned flour
50 g (2 oz) dripping
2 onions, skinned
1 carrot, pared
½ turnip, peeled
1 bayleaf
pinch dried parsley or a few fresh parsley stalks
2·5 ml (½ level tsp) dried thyme or 7·5 ml (1½ level tsps) chopped fresh thyme
2·5 ml (½ level tsp) dried marjoram, or 7·5 ml (1½ level tsps) chopped fresh marjoram
300 ml (½ pt) beef stock
salt and pepper
chopped parsley to garnish

Serves 4–6

Wash the ox heart in cold water, drain it and trim off the flaps, lobes and any gristle. Cut it into 0·5-cm (¼-in) slices and cut each slice in half. Coat them with flour, then brown in hot dripping (a single layer at a time in a frying pan). Lift out and keep on one side. Finely slice the onions, carrot and turnip and add these to the pan, cover and cook for 10 minutes. Stir in the herbs and stock, loosen the sediment from the pan, then return the heart slices and adjust the seasoning. Turn it all into a casserole, cover and cook in the oven at 150°C (300°F) mark 1–2 for about 2½ hours. Discard the bayleaf and parsley stalks. Garnish with parsley just before serving.

*Spicy red curry

40 g (1½ oz) margarine or butter
30 ml (2 tbsps) dried onion flakes or 1
  large onion, skinned and chopped
396-g (14-oz) can tomatoes
large pinch crushed chilies
pinch grated whole ginger
1·25 ml (¼ level tsp) chili seasoning
4 cloves
large pinch ground cinnamon
8 cardamom seeds, crushed
large pinch turmeric
5 ml (1 level tsp) salt
4 chicken portions

Serves 4

Melt the fat in a pan, add the fresh
onion and fry until soft – do not
brown. Add tomatoes and their juice,
dried onions and the spices and salt;
cover and cook gently for 15–20 minutes.

Add the chicken portions, one by
one, turning them in the sauce. Cover
and simmer gently for about 45 minutes
– 1 hour, or until fork tender. Serve
with yoghurt, mango chutney and pop-
padoms.

Kidney ragout

15 ml (1 tbsp) dried onion flakes or
  1 medium onion, skinned and chopped
50 g (2 oz) butter
4–6 sheeps kidneys
45 ml (3 level tbsps) flour
300 ml (½ pt) beef stock
1 bouquet garni
15 ml (1 level tbsp) tomato paste
15 ml (1 level tbsp) dried sweet pepper
  flakes
salt and pepper
50 g (2 oz) mushrooms, wiped and sliced

Serves 2–3

If you are using dried onion, soak it in
warm water for 10 minutes, then drain
it. Melt the butter and fry the onion
until golden brown. Wash, skin and
core the kidneys and cut them into
pieces, add to the pan and cook for 5
minutes, stirring occasionally. Stir in
the flour, pour in the stock and bring
slowly to the boil, then add the bouquet
garni, tomato paste, pepper flakes and
seasoning. Simmer for 5 minutes. Add
the mushrooms and simmer for a further
5 minutes. Remove the bouquet garni,
adjust the seasoning and serve with
boiled rice.

*Somerset tripe

30 ml (2 tbsps) dried onion flakes or 2
  medium onions, skinned and chopped
1 kg (2 lb) prepared tripe
90 ml (6 tbsps) oil
1 bayleaf
150 ml (¼ pt) dry cider
184-g (6½-oz) can tomatoes
1·25 ml (¼ level tsp) garlic granules or
  1 clove garlic, skinned and finely
  chopped
pinch of dried rosemary and grated nutmeg
5 ml (1 level tsp) dried parsley or 15 ml
  (1 tbsp) chopped fresh parsley
15 ml (1 level tbsp) beef extract
150 ml (¼ pt) water
salt and ground black pepper
chopped fresh parsley for garnish

Serves 6

If you are using dried onion, soak it in
warm water for 10 minutes, then drain it.
Cut the tripe into fine strips. Fry the
onion (fresh or dried) in the oil until
golden, then add the bayleaf and cider.
Cover the pan and cook slowly until
the cider is well reduced. Add the tripe,

tomatoes with juice, garlic, rosemary, nutmeg, parsley and beef extract dissolved in water. Season with salt and pepper, cover and cook gently for 1 hour. Remove the tripe from the juices, using a draining spoon, and keep it warm. Reduce the juices by fast boiling to 300 ml ($\frac{1}{2}$ pt). Return the tripe to the pan and reheat it. Serve with more parsley scattered on top.

Liver in savoury sauce

15 ml (1 tbsp) dried onion flakes or 1 medium onion, skinned and chopped
450 g (1 lb) lamb's liver, sliced
50 g (2 oz) butter
225 g (8 oz) courgettes, trimmed and sliced
10 ml (2 level tsps) flour
150 ml ($\frac{1}{4}$ pt) light stock
150 ml (5 fl oz) single cream
15 ml (1 tbsp) lemon juice
5 ml (1 level tsp) dried marjoram or 15 ml (1 tbsp) chopped fresh marjoram
4 tomatoes, skinned and quartered
salt and ground black pepper
bacon-flavoured potato crisps

Serves 4

Soak the dried onion in 15 ml (1 tbsp) warm water for 10 minutes then drain it. Cube the liver. Melt 25 g (1 oz) butter in an oven-to-table flameproof casserole, sauté the onion in it until beginning to soften, then add the courgettes and cook for 5 minutes. Keep on one side. Add 25 g (1 oz) butter to the pan, sauté the liver to seal, stir in the flour and cook for 1–2 minutes. Add the stock, cream, lemon juice, herbs and tomatoes, stirring. Return the onion/courgette mixture to the pan, adjust the seasoning with salt and pepper and bring to serving temperature. To serve, top with a good layer of roughly crushed potato crisps.

Herb-stuffed haddock fillet

2 fillets of fresh haddock, each about 350 g ($\frac{3}{4}$ lb)
1 large tomato, sliced
50 g (2 oz) butter or margarine, melted
5 ml (1 tsp) dried parsley or 15 ml (1 tbsp) chopped fresh parsley

For herb stuffing

100 g (4 oz) fresh white breadcrumbs
large knob of margarine
1 rasher bacon, rinded and chopped
1 large stick celery, trimmed and finely chopped
15 ml (1 level tbsp) dried minced onion
10 ml (2 tsps) dried parsley or 30 ml (2 tbsps) chopped fresh parsley
1·25 ml ($\frac{1}{4}$ level tsp) celery salt
15 ml (1 tbsp) lemon juice
pinch of pepper
pinch of dried tarragon or 5 ml (1 tsp) chopped fresh tarragon
1 large egg, beaten

Serves 4

Wash and dry the fish, leaving the skin on. Place 1 fillet, flesh side uppermost, in a buttered shallow ovenproof dish.

Put the breadcrumbs in a bowl. Heat the margarine in a small pan, add the bacon and celery and fry until soft. Add to the breadcrumbs with the remaining stuffing ingredients and mix them thoroughly. Cover the fillet with stuffing. Put the second fillet, skin side uppermost, on top. Lay tomato slices on top, coat with melted butter and sprinkle with the remaining parsley. Bake uncovered in the oven at 180°C (350°F) mark 4 for about 40 minutes.

* Seafood creole

1 small green pepper, seeded and finely
 chopped
5 ml (1 tsp) onion flakes or 1 small
 onion, skinned and finely chopped
40 g (1½ oz) butter
450 g (1 lb) fillet of cod, haddock or whit-
 ing, skinned
45 ml (3 level tbsps) flour
396-g (14-oz) and a 225-g (8-oz) can
 tomatoes
2·5 ml (½ level tsp) dried rosemary or
 7·5 ml (1½ tsps) chopped fresh rosemary
2·5 ml (½ level tsp) dried thyme or 7·5
 ml (1½ tsps) chopped fresh thyme
2·5 ml (½ level tsp) dried oregano
large pinch of chili seasoning
salt and pepper
5 ml (1 level tsp) sugar
100 g (4 oz) peeled prawns

Serves 4

Fry the pepper and fresh onion in 25 g
(1 oz) butter for 5 minutes until soft,
then drain and remove them from the
pan. Wash and dry the fish, cut it into
2·5-cm (1-in) cubes. Toss the fish pieces
in the flour and fry for 2–3 minutes, then
remove from the pan. Melt the remaining butter, add any remaining flour and
gradually stir in the tomatoes and their
juice, pepper mixture, herbs, chili
seasoning, dried onion if used, salt,
pepper and sugar. Cover and simmer

gently for 10 minutes until the sauce has
thickened and flavours have blended.
Add the fish and prawns and cook for a
further 5 minutes. Serve with boiled rice.

Cod cutlets in mush-
room cream sauce

15 ml (1 tbsp) dried onion flakes or 1
 medium onion, skinned and chopped
50 g (2 oz) butter
4 cod cutlets
175 g (6 oz) mushrooms, wiped and
 sliced
salt and pepper
150 ml (5 fl oz) soured cream
pinch dried basil
fish seasoning
freshly chopped chives

Serves 4

Soak dried onion in 15 ml (1 tbsp) warm
water for 10 minutes. Drain. Melt
some butter in a pan and cook the fish
until tender. Meanwhile prepare the
sauce. Gently cook the onions and mushrooms in the hot butter for 2 minutes.
Season with salt and pepper, pour in the
soured cream and add the basil and fish
seasoning to taste. Heat gently until the
sauce is really hot but not boiling. Place
the cutlets on a hot serving dish and
pour the sauce over. Sprinkle with
chopped chives.

Pickled meat

Silverside or brisket of beef, leg or belly of pork, ox tongue and pig's head are particularly suited to pickling or salting. The only equipment required is a large earthenware crock, bowl or basin or a polythene bowl or pail, with a board or lid to keep out the dust. Home pickling is best done in cold weather. Trim and wash the meat, then rub it over with salt to remove all traces of blood.

Of the two methods given below, the first is the easier, but the second gives a more interesting flavour to the meat.

Wet pickle
Put 4·5 l (1 gal) water, 700 g (1½ lb) bay or common salt, 25 g (1 oz) salt-petre and 175 g (6 oz) brown sugar in a large pan, bring to the boil and boil for 15–20 minutes, skimming carefully. Strain the liquid into the container you are using, allow to cool, put in the meat and cover.

Dry pickle
Pound 225 g (½ lb) bay salt, mix with 225 g (½ lb) common salt, 225 g (½ lb) brown sugar, 20 ml (4 level tsps) salt-petre, 20 ml (4 level tsps) black pepper and 5 ml (1 level tsp) allspice. Rub the meat daily with this mixture, leaving it meantime in the covered container.

Pickling time
A thick cut of beef needs about 10 days, whereas a thinner cut, or a pig's head split in half, may be sufficiently salted in 4–5 days.

Cooking pickled meat

Remove the meat from the pickle and wash it thoroughly in cold water. If you wish, soak it for 1 hour in cold water before cooking. Tie the meat up neatly if necessary, put it into a pan of cold water, bring slowly to the boil and skim. Add some sliced carrot, turnip and onion, a few peppercorns and a bouquet garni and let the water simmer very gently until the meat is tender: allow 1 hour per 450 g (1 lb) for joints up to 1·4 kg (3 lb) or a total of 3–4 hours for joints weighing 1·8 kg–2·3 kg (4–5 lb). (The liquid may be used for making soups.)

Party Dinners

Steak with fines herbes

4 steaks (175 g–225 g, 6–8 oz each), see
   recipe
meat tenderizer, optional – 1·25 ml ($\frac{1}{4}$
   level tsp) for each steak
salt
freshly ground pepper
75 g (3 oz) butter
15 ml (1 tbsp) oil
2·5 ml ($\frac{1}{2}$ level tsp) each of dried chives
   and parsley or 7·5 ml (1$\frac{1}{2}$ tsps) chopped
   fresh chives and parsley or 5 ml (1
   level tsp) dried *fines herbes*

Serves 4

If a tender rump steak is used no tenderizer is necessary, but for an economical
tasty steak buy slices of braising or
top side steak, and use tenderizer.

   Sprinkle the meat with tenderizer if
necessary, and leave for 30 minutes.
Cook the steaks in 40 g (1$\frac{1}{2}$ oz) butter,
as for pepper steak (below). Remove the
steaks from the pan. Add the remaining
butter and herbs and stir until the butter
has melted. Pour the sauce over the meat
and serve immediately.

* Pepper steak

4 steaks (175 g–225 g, 6–8 oz each), see
   previous recipe
meat tenderizer, optional – 1·25 ml ($\frac{1}{4}$
   level tsp) for each steak
15–30 ml (1–2 level tbsps) coarsely ground
   black peppercorns
50 g (2 oz) butter
15 ml (1 tbsp) olive oil
salt
10 ml (2 tsps) brandy
150 ml ($\frac{1}{4}$ pt) beef stock
30 ml (2 tbsps) double cream

Serves 4

Ask the butcher to flatten the steaks or
place them between two sheets of greaseproof paper and beat well until thin.
Sprinkle the steaks with meat tenderizer
(if necessary) and press the crushed
peppercorns well into each side of the
meat. Leave for 30 minutes if using
tenderizer. Heat the butter and oil in a
pan, fry the steaks for 3–4 minutes each
side, season with salt, remove from the
pan and keep warm. Add the brandy to
the pan with the stock and cook over
high heat until the stock is reduced by
half. Add the cream. Pour over the
steaks and serve at once.

Pork stroganoff

4 spare rib chops
30 ml (2 tbsps) corn oil
salt and ground pepper
30 ml (2 tbsps) dried onion flakes or 2
   medium onions, skinned and chopped
5 ml (1 level tsp) dried sage
425-g (15-oz) can consommé
225 g (8 oz) button mushrooms, wiped
50 g (2 oz) butter
150 ml (5 fl oz) soured cream
chopped fresh parsley

Serves 4

Wipe the meat with a damp cloth.
Brush both sides of each chop with oil.
Season well and quickly brown the
chops on both sides in a frying pan. Drain
them before placing in a shallow casserole dish. If you are using dried onion
flakes, soak them in warm water for
10 minutes, then drain them.

   Reheat the pan juices, quickly fry the
onions (fresh or dried) to colour them,
then drain and put on one side. Mix the
sage with the consommé, pour it over
the meat, cover and cook in the oven at
170°C (325°F) mark 3 for 2$\frac{1}{4}$ hours.

Add the onions after $1\frac{1}{4}$ hours. Slice the mushrooms, melt the butter and gently sauté them until they are soft.

Drain the juices from the casserole into a saucepan. Keep the pork warm in the oven. Skim off any excess fat from the juices, add the mushrooms and rapidly boil to reduce the liquid to 300 ml ($\frac{1}{2}$ pt). Pour it over the meat. Stir the soured cream with a spoon to give an even consistency. Spoon it over the meat and heat through in the oven for 5–10 minutes before serving, liberally scattered with chopped parsley.

Sugar glazed gammon

1·6 kg ($3\frac{1}{2}$ lb) corner or middle gammon
1 small onion, skinned and sliced
2 small carrots, pared and quartered
1 bayleaf
4 peppercorns
whole cloves
2·5 ml ($\frac{1}{2}$ level tsp) mustard seeds
pinch ground ginger
60 ml (4 level tbsps) soft brown sugar
60 ml (4 tbsps) milk

Serves 8

Weigh the gammon and calculate the cooking time, allowing 20–25 minutes per 450 g (1 lb) plus 20 minutes over.

Place the gammon in a large pan, cover with cold water and add the onion, carrot, bayleaf and peppercorns. Bring slowly to the boil, skimming off any scum that forms. Time the cooking from this point. Boil it gently for half the cooking time, then drain the joint and wrap in foil. Bake in the oven at 180°C (350°F) mark 4, until 30 minutes before cooking time is finished. Raise the oven heat to 220°C (425°F) mark 7. Undo the foil, peel off the rind from the bacon, score the fat into diamonds with a sharp knife and stud with cloves. Crush the mustard seeds with a rolling pin and mix them with the ginger, sugar and milk. Pour this over the gammon. Return the joint to the oven until crisp and golden, basting frequently with the milk mixture during cooking. Serve hot or cold.

* Lamb kebabs

900 g (2 lb) boned leg of lamb
1 lemon, for garnish

Eastern marinade
90 ml (6 tbsps) olive oil
60 ml (4 tbsps) lemon juice
1·25 ml ($\frac{1}{4}$ level tsp) garlic granules or 1 clove garlic, skinned and crushed
salt and freshly ground black pepper
5 ml (1 level tsp) dried onion flakes or 1 small onion, skinned and finely chopped
10 ml (2 level tsps) dried parsley or 30 ml (2 tbsps) finely chopped fresh parsley
2·5 ml ($\frac{1}{2}$ level tsp) dried oregano

Moroccan marinade
$\frac{1}{2}$ leek (white end), washed and very finely chopped
15 ml (1 tbsp) dried onion flakes or 1 medium onion, skinned and finely chopped
5 ml (1 level tsp) dried chervil or 15 ml (1 tbsp) chopped fresh chervil
5 ml (1 level tsp) salt
5 ml (1 level tsp) ground black pepper
5 ml (1 level tsp) ground ginger
5 ml (1 level tsp) ground cumin
1·25 ml ($\frac{1}{4}$ level tsp) paprika
1·25 ml ($\frac{1}{4}$ level tsp) cayenne pepper
90 ml (tbsps) olive oil

Serves 6

Cut the lamb into 2·5-cm (1-in) cubes.

Choose one of the marinades and combine the ingredients together. Add the meat to the marinade mixture and mix well, making sure each piece of meat is properly covered. Cover the bowl and leave for at least 2 hours (or preferably overnight). When ready to cook, thread the meat on to skewers, brush with the marinade and cook under a medium grill for 12–15 minutes, turning the kebabs about 3 times, until the meat is tender. Serve on boiled rice, with lemon wedges

Other additions can be made to the kebabs – these may be cubed green pepper, a few bayleaves, quartered onions, button mushrooms or tomato halves. Thread these on to the skewers alternating with the meat (do not add to the marinade).

* West Indian lamb

10 ml (2 tsps) dried onion flakes, or 1
  small onion, skinned and chopped
900 g (2 lb) boned shoulder of lamb
25 g (1 oz) butter
15 ml (1 tbsp) oil
7·5–15 ml ($\frac{1}{2}$–1 level tbsp) curry powder
2·5 ml ($\frac{1}{2}$ level tsp) turmeric
1·25 ml ($\frac{1}{4}$ level tsp) cayenne pepper
pinch ground ginger
salt and freshly ground black pepper
45 ml (3 tbsps) lemon juice
300 ml ($\frac{1}{2}$ pt) chicken stock
15 ml (1 level tbsp) desiccated coconut

Serves 6

If you are using dried onion flakes, soak them in warm water for 10 minutes, then drain and set them aside. Remove any excess fat from the lamb and cut the meat into 4-cm (1$\frac{1}{2}$-in) cubes. Melt the butter and oil in a pan, add the meat

and onions and fry gently on all sides until golden. Stir in the spices, seasonings and lemon juice. Mix well, then gradually add the stock and onion. Cover the pan and simmer gently for 1$\frac{1}{2}$–2 hours or until the meat is tender. Turn into a warm serving dish and sprinkle with the coconut. Serve with boiled rice and chutneys.

Apricot stuffed lamb with rosemary

2 kg (4$\frac{1}{2}$ lb) leg of lamb, boned

For marinade
5 ml (1 level tsp) dried rosemary or 15 ml
  (1 tbsp) chopped fresh rosemary
90 ml (6 tbsps) oil
60 ml (4 tbsps) lemon juice

For stuffing
15 ml (1 tbsp) dried onion flakes or 1
  medium onion, skinned and chopped
large knob of lard
4 rashers streaky bacon, rinded and
  chopped
175 g (6 oz) cooked rice (about 50 g, 2 oz,
  raw)
1 stick celery, trimmed and chopped
50 g (2 oz) dried apricots, chopped
30 ml (2 tbsps) sultanas
5 ml (1 level tsp) dried rosemary or 15 ml
  (1 tbsp) chopped fresh rosemary
celery salt
freshly ground black pepper
1 small egg, beaten

Serves 8

Put the meat into a shallow ovenproof dish, just large enough to take the joint. Mix the marinade ingredients together, pour over the meat, cover and leave for 2–3 hours, or overnight if possible, turning occasionally.

Prepare the stuffing. If you are using dried onion, soak it in warm water for 10 minutes and then drain. Heat the lard, fry the bacon in a small pan, add the fresh onion and cook until soft. Add to the rice with the celery, apricots, sultanas, herbs, seasoning, dried onion if you are using it and egg to bind.

Remove the meat from the marinade. Stuff the cavity with the rice stuffing and sew it up with a trussing needle and fine string. Return the meat to the dish. Cook it in the oven at 180°C (350°F) mark 4, for 2 hours 10 minutes, basting occasionally during cooking with the surplus marinade. Place the meat on a hot serving plate, remove the excess fat from the juices in the pan and serve the juices separately. Serve with green vegetables.

Escalopes fines herbes

50 g (2 oz) butter
4 escalopes of veal
75 ml (5 level tbsps) flour
salt and pepper
10 ml (2 level tsps) tomato paste
150 ml ($\frac{1}{4}$ pt) red wine
100 g (4 oz) button mushrooms, wiped and sliced
2·5 ml ($\frac{1}{2}$ level tsp) dried mixed herbs
150 ml (5 fl oz) single cream
350 g (12 oz) tomatoes
50 g (2 oz) cheese, grated
sliced tomato for garnish, optional

Serves 4

Heat the butter in a frying pan. Roll the escalopes up tightly and secure each with a cocktail stick. Mix half the flour with some salt and pepper and toss the meat in this. Cook the escalopes gently in the fat for 7–10 minutes, turning them frequently until evenly browned. Re-

move them from the pan, drain and keep hot. Add the remaining flour to the pan, stir in the tomato paste and wine and bring slowly to the boil; add the mushrooms, herbs and lastly the cream, season as required and cook very gently, without boiling, for 5 minutes. Peel and chop the tomatoes, discarding the seeds. Put them into a dish, put the meat on top, pour the sauce over, sprinkle with the cheese and brown under the grill. Garnish if you wish with another sliced tomato.

Veal goulash with caraway dumplings

700 g ($1\frac{1}{2}$ lb) boned shoulder of veal
30 ml (2 tbsps) cooking oil
4 medium onions
1·25 ml ($\frac{1}{4}$ level tsp) garlic salt
5 ml (1 level tsp) salt
pepper
6 medium tomatoes, skinned and sliced
stock
150 ml (5 fl oz) soured cream
10 ml (2 level tsps) paprika
5 ml (1 level tsp) caraway seeds
chopped parsley

Serves 4–5

Cut the meat into 4-cm ($1\frac{1}{2}$-in) cubes and sauté in the hot oil until they are lightly browned. Skin, slice and fry the onions, add the garlic salt, salt and pepper and the tomatoes. Pour on just enough stock to cover the meat and vegetables, bring to the boil, cover and simmer gently for $1\frac{1}{2}$ hours or until the meat is tender, stirring occasionally. Remove the meat and keep it hot. Reduce the sauce to half by fast boiling. Add the paprika and caraway seeds, cover and simmer very gently for 30 minutes.

Meanwhile prepare the dumplings – see below. Return the meat to the sauce, add the soured cream and parsley and heat through slowly, without boiling. Serve with the dumplings.

Caraway dumplings

100 g (4 oz) plain flour
5 ml (1 level tsp) baking powder
2·5 ml ($\frac{1}{2}$ level tsp) salt
5 ml (1 level tsp) caraway seeds
pepper
40 g (1$\frac{1}{2}$ oz) fat
cold water

Mix the dry ingredients and rub in the fat with the fingertips. Mix to a firm, light dough with cold water, divide into 8 or 10 equal-sized portions, roll into balls and cook in boiling water for about 25 minutes.

Saltimbocca

8 thin slices of veal, about 50 g (2 oz) per
　　slice
8 thin slices of lean ham
7·5 ml (1$\frac{1}{2}$ level tsps) dried sage or 8 fresh
　　sage leaves
salt and freshly ground black pepper
50 g (2 oz) butter
60 ml (4 tbsps) dry white wine
croûtons of fried bread

Serves 4

Beat out the veal slices with a heavy rolling pin until they are about 10 by 12·5 cm (4 by 5 in). On each lay a slice of ham. Sprinkle lightly with dried sage or lay a sage leaf on each slice. Season with salt and pepper. Make each slice into a small roll and secure with a wooden cocktail stick. Heat the butter in a frying pan and fry the veal rolls

until golden. Add the wine, adjust the seasoning, and simmer gently until the veal rolls are tender – about 12–15 minutes. Serve the veal with croûtons of fried bread.

* Escalope de veau au poivre rose

4 veal escalopes, about 150 g (5 oz) each
15 ml (1 tbsp) oil
25 g (1 oz) butter
15 ml (1 level tbsp) flour
5 ml (1 level tsp) paprika
2 bayleaves
1 lemon
salt and freshly ground black pepper
60 ml (4 tbsps) double cream
lemon wedges for garnish

Serves 4

Bat out the escalopes and nick the edges to prevent the meat contracting. Heat the the oil in a wide, shallow, flameproof casserole. When it is hot, add the butter. Coat the escalopes in the sifted flour and paprika. When the butter is sizzling, add the escalopes and quickly cook on one side only until golden brown. Remove the escalopes, retain the meat juices and drain off the fat. Add the bayleaves to the pan with the thinly pared rind of half a lemon and 15 ml (1 tbsp) lemon juice and salt and pepper. Replace the escalopes, golden side uppermost, in the pan. Cover with a tightly fitting lid and simmer very gently on the top of the stove for 20 minutes. Remove the escalopes and keep them warm. Reduce the pan juices to about 45 ml (3 tbsps), stir in the cream a little at a time, gently reheat without boiling and adjust the seasoning. Replace the escalopes, heat through and garnish with lemon wedges.

Poulet-salami basquais

50 g (2 oz) lard
4 large joints of chicken
1 onion, skinned and sliced
1·25 ml ($\frac{1}{4}$ level tsp) dried thyme
1 bayleaf
strip of orange rind
175 g (6 oz) piece of salami
salt and pepper
600 ml (1 pt) chicken stock
225 g ($\frac{1}{2}$ lb) tomatoes, skinned and chopped
10 ml (2 level tsps) dried sweet pepper flakes
15 ml (1 level tbsp) paprika
225 g (8 oz) long grain rice

Serves 4

Melt 25 g (1 oz) lard in a large saucepan and brown the chicken well on all sides. Remove the joints from the pan. Add the onion to the pan and fry for a few minutes. Replace the chicken, tie the thyme, bayleaf and orange rind in a small piece of muslin and add this to the pan with the salami in one piece, salt and pepper. Pour on the stock, cover and simmer for about 40 minutes or until the chicken is tender.

Strain off the stock and discard the muslin bag. Keep the chicken and salami hot and reduce the stock to one third by fast boiling. Melt the remaining lard in a fresh pan, add the tomatoes, pepper flakes, paprika and reduced chicken stock. Boil uncovered until the sauce is reduced to a coating consistency, then adjust the seasoning. Meanwhile cook the rice in boiling salted water until tender, then drain it. Arrange it on a hot dish, top with the chicken joints and pour the sauce over. Skin and slice the cooked salami and use it to garnish the chicken.

Chicken with fresh peaches in barbecue sauce

4 chicken portions
25 g (1 oz) butter, melted
10 ml (2 tsps) clear honey
10 ml (2 level tsps) Dijon mustard
15 ml (1 tbsp) Worcestershire sauce
75 ml (5 tbsps) vinegar
1·25 ml ($\frac{1}{4}$ level tsp) chili seasoning
1·25 ml ($\frac{1}{4}$ level tsp) dried marjoram
2 fresh peaches
10 ml (2 level tsps) cornflour

Serves 4

Brush the chicken portions with butter and place them in a baking dish. Combine all the ingredients except the peaches and cornflour and pour them over the chicken. Cook in the oven at 190°C (375°F) mark 5 for about 1 hour, basting frequently. Skin and quarter the peaches; add them to the chicken for the last 15 minutes of the cooking time.

Pour off the juices into a saucepan and skim off the fat. Blend the cornflour to a cream with a little cold water, stir it into the pan juices and bring to the boil, stirring. Pour the thickened juices over the chicken and re-heat in the oven to serving temperature.

Duckling, apple and celery casserole

15 ml (1 tbsp) dried onion flakes or 1 medium onion, skinned and chopped

1·8-kg (4-lb) oven ready duckling

25 g (1 oz) butter

2 sticks celery, trimmed and chopped

1 large cooking apple, peeled, cored and chopped

15 ml (1 level tbsp) flour

300 ml ($\frac{1}{2}$ pt) dry cider

5 ml (1 level tsp) dried sage or 15 ml (1 tbsp) chopped fresh sage

celery salt

pepper

Serves 4

If you are using dried onion, soak it in warm water to cover for 10 minutes, then drain. Cut the duckling into four joints. Cut away the skin and excess fat and wash and dry the joints. Heat the butter, then fry the duckling on all sides until golden. Drain the joints well and remove any further traces of fat using kitchen paper. Place them in a casserole.

Drain off all but 15 ml (1 tbsp) fat from the pan, add the onion (fresh or dried) celery and apple, and fry gently until pale golden. Stir in the flour. Remove the pan from the heat and gradually stir in the cider. Return it to the heat, bring to the boil, add the sage, celery salt and pepper to taste. Pour the sauce over the duckling, cover the casserole and cook in the oven at 180°C (350°F) mark 4, for about 1$\frac{1}{2}$ hours or until the meat is tender.

* Devilled grilled turkey

2 turkey breasts, about 450 g (1 lb)

5 ml (1 level tsp) salt

10 ml (2 level tsps) sugar

5 ml (1 level tsp) ground pepper

5 ml (1 level tsp) ground ginger

5 ml (1 level tsp) dry mustard

2·5 ml ($\frac{1}{2}$ level tsp) curry powder

25 g (1 oz) butter, melted

For sauce

25 g (1 oz) butter, melted

30 ml (2 level tbsps) tomato paste

15 ml (1 tbsp) vinegar

15 ml (1 tbsp) cold water

10 ml (2 tsps) Worcestershire sauce

15 ml (1 tbsp) soy sauce

1·25 ml ($\frac{1}{4}$ level tsp) chili seasoning

Serves 4

Slice the turkey breasts to give 4 thin escalope shapes. Mix the salt, sugar, pepper, ginger, mustard and curry powder together, rub the mixture into the turkey portions and leave for 1 hour. Brush them with the melted butter, place in a grill pan and grill them slowly until brown – about 8 minutes each side.

Mix the sauce ingredients together then spoon them over the turkey. Continue to cook, basting with the sauce, for 6 minutes. Serve on a hot dish with boiled rice.

Bramble syllabub ▶

Casserole of rabbit with juniper berries

corn oil
1 kg (2½ lb) rabbit pieces
60 ml (4 level tbsps) flour
30 ml (2 level tbsps) tomato paste
300 ml (½ pt) rich brown stock
150 ml (¼ pt) red wine
1 bouquet garni
2 bayleaves
5 ml (1 level tsp) salt
ground black pepper
8 juniper berries
1·25 ml (¼ level tsp) garlic granules or 1
   clove garlic, skinned and crushed
225 g (8 oz) back bacon rashers, rinded
croûtons of fried bread

Serves 4–6

Heat 45 ml (3 tbsps) oil and quickly brown the rabbit pieces and place them in a large casserole. Add the flour and tomato paste to the pan juices, cook for 1–2 minutes then stir in the stock and wine. Add the herbs and seasoning. Lightly crush the berries and add them to the pan with the garlic. Bring to the boil and cook for 2 minutes. Pour the sauce over the rabbit. Cover it and cook in the oven at 170°C (325°F) mark 3 for 2–2½ hours or until tender.

Stretch the bacon rashers with the back of a knife. Halve them and make into rolls. Thread them on skewers and grill until crisp. Take the rolls off the skewers and fold them through the casserole 30 minutes before the end of the cooking time. Garnish with croûtons to serve.

* Lemon fish kebabs

700–900 g (1½–2 lb) fillet of halibut or
   other firm white fish

For marinade
30 ml (2 tbsps) oil
30 ml (2 tbsps) lemon juice
2·5 ml (½ level tsp) grated lemon rind
pinch of garlic salt
salt and pepper
pinch of ground ginger
5 ml (1 level tsp) dried rosemary or 15 ml
   (1 tbsp) chopped fresh rosemary
8 dried or fresh bay leaves, halved
fish seasoning

Serves 4–6

Wash and dry the fish, leaving the skin on. Cut it into 2·5-cm (1-in) cubes and place them in a shallow dish. Mix the marinade ingredients together, pour over the fish, cover and refrigerate for at least ½ hour.

Thread the fish and pieces of bayleaf on to skewers, strain the marinade and brush it over the kebabs; sprinkle with fish seasoning. Grill slowly for about 10 minutes until the fish is cooked, turning and basting occasionally with the marinade during cooking. Serve with fresh green vegetables.

◀ *Minted fruit fingers; Orange cinnamon crisps; Easter spice biscuits; Sesame seed crescents; Aniseed biscuits; Apple shortcakes*

Suppers

Spaghetti bolognese

30 ml (2 tbsps) dried onion flakes or
   1 large onion, skinned and chopped
15 ml (1 tbsp) oil
700 g (1½ lb) beef, minced
2·5 ml (½ level tsp) dried basil
2·5 ml (½ level tsp) chili seasoning
5 ml (1 level tsp) paprika
salt and pepper
396-g (14-oz) and a 226-g (8-oz) can of
   tomatoes
100 g (4 oz) Cheddar cheese, grated

Serves 4–6

Soak the onion flakes in warm water
for 10 minutes, then drain. Heat the
oil and sauté the onion until clear, then
add the beef and brown it. Add the
basil, spices, salt, pepper and tomatoes,
with their juice. Cover and simmer very
gently for 30–45 minutes. Serve on a
bed of spaghetti, sprinkled with grated
cheese.

*Spinach layer pie

30 ml (2 tbsps) dried onion flakes or 1
   large onion, skinned and chopped
450 g (1 lb) lean beef, minced
30 ml (2 level tbsps) tomato paste
5 ml (1 level tsp) dried mixed herbs
salt and freshly ground pepper
450 g (1 lb) frozen chopped spinach
pinch of nutmeg
300 ml (½ pt) natural yoghurt
2 egg yolks
pinch dry mustard
50 g (2 oz) Edam cheese, grated

Serves 4

Soak the onion flakes in warm water for
10 minutes, then drain them. Put the
minced beef and onions in a large saucepan and cook over a medium heat until
the fat starts to run; increase the heat
and brown the meat. Stir in the tomato
paste, herbs and seasoning. Place the
spinach in a saucepan without water,
cover and cook it gently until the
spinach has thawed. Drain it very
thoroughly and stir in nutmeg, salt and
pepper to taste.

Layer the meat mixture and the
spinach in an ovenproof dish. Combine
the yoghurt, egg yolks, mustard and
cheese. Pour these over the top of the
casserole and cook in the oven, uncovered, at 190°C (375°F) mark 5,
for about 45 minutes until the topping is
bubbling and golden.

Bacon and potato layer

90 ml (6 tbsps) soured cream
45 ml (3 tbsps) double cream
5 ml (1 level tsp) salt
5 ml (1 level tsp) dried mixed herbs
125 g (4½ oz) butter
700 g (1½ lb) cold cooked potatoes, thinly
   sliced
4 hardboiled eggs, sliced
275 g (10 oz) back bacon rashers, rinded,
   lightly grilled and roughly chopped
75 g (3 oz) fresh breadcrumbs
2·5 ml (½ level tsp) celery salt

Serves 4

Put the soured cream, double cream,
salt and herbs in a bowl and mix them
together. Grease the inside of an ovenproof dish with 40 g (1½ oz) butter, then
put in one third of the potatoes; cover
with the sliced eggs and pour some of
the cream mixture over. Add another
third of the potatoes in a layer. Lay the
bacon over the potatoes, then pour the
remaining cream mixture over. Top
with the remaining slices of potato.
Mix the breadcrumbs and celery salt

with the remaining melted butter and sprinkle this over the potatoes. Bake in the oven at 190°C (375°F) mark 5 for 30–40 minutes, or until top is golden.

* Cheese and parsley soufflé

3 large eggs
25 g (1 oz) butter
20 ml (1½ level tbsps) flour
150 ml (¼ pt) milk
75 g (3 oz) Cheddar cheese, grated
2·5 ml (½ level tsp) dry mustard
10 ml (2 level tsps) dried parsley or 30 ml
   (2 tbsps) chopped fresh parsley
salt and pepper
cayenne pepper

Serves 2

Grease an 18-cm (7-in) soufflé dish and separate the eggs. Melt the butter, stir in the flour and cook for 2–3 minutes. Gradually stir in the milk and bring to the boil, stirring all the time, then let it cool slightly. Add the egg yolks one at a time, beating well. Stir in the cheese, mustard, parsley, salt and pepper.

Stiffly whisk the egg whites and fold these into the mixture. Turn it into the soufflé dish and sprinkle very lightly with cayenne. Bake in the oven at 200°C (400°F) mark 6 for about 35 minutes until well risen and brown.

* Herb omelette

2 large eggs
15 ml (1 tbsp) cold water
salt and pepper
5 ml (1 level tsp) dried *fines herbes*
large knob of butter

Serves 1

Whisk the eggs, water, seasoning and herbs together. Melt the butter in a frying or omelette pan over a moderate heat, tilting the pan so that the inside surface is evenly greased. Pour in the egg mixture and gently stir with a fork, the back of the prongs held flat against the base of the pan, until the uncooked egg has set. Stop stirring and cook the omelette for another minute until the underside is golden brown. Using a palette knife, fold the omelette by flicking one third over to the centre, then folding over the opposite side. Turn the omelette on to a heated plate with the folded side undermost. Serve at once.

The following are delicious when added to the eggs before cooking as an alternative to *fines herbes*:
1. 5 ml (1 level tsp) dried mixed herbs
2. 5 ml (1 level tsp) dried parsley or 15 ml (1 tbsp) chopped fresh parsley
3. pinch dried rosemary or 2·5 ml (½ tsp) fresh rosemary
4. 5 ml (1 level tsp) dried chives or 15 ml (1 tbsp) chopped fresh chives
5. 5 ml (1 level tsp) dried marjoram or 15 ml (1 tbsp) chopped fresh marjoram

* Italian tomato omelette

10 ml (2 tsps) dried sweet pepper flakes
5 ml (1 level tsp) dried minced onion
large knob of butter
2 tomatoes, skinned and chopped
1·25 ml (¼ level tsp) Italian seasoning
2 eggs
15 ml (1 tbsp) cold water
salt and pepper
large knob of butter

Serves 1

Soak the pepper flakes and onion in hot water for 10 minutes and then drain well. In a small pan, heat the butter and when melted add the pepper flakes, tomato, onion and Italian seasoning. Cook gently until soft and of a fairly thick consistency, keep hot. Prepare the omelette as for herb omelette but omit the herbs. Put the hot filling over the cooked omelette before folding. Serve at once.

Savoury cheese flan

For herb pastry
150 g (5 oz) plain flour
1·25 ml ($\frac{1}{4}$ level tsp) salt
2·5 ml ($\frac{1}{2}$ level tsp) dried mixed herbs
75 g (3 oz) fat, half butter or margarine and half lard

For filling
15 ml (1 tbsp) dried onion flakes or 1 medium onion, skinned and chopped
15 ml (1 tbsp) oil
100 g (4 oz) cheese, grated
5 ml (1 level tsp) dried chives or 15 ml (1 tbsp) chopped fresh chives
2 large eggs
150 ml ($\frac{1}{4}$ pt) milk
salt and pepper

Serves 4

Sift the flour and salt into a bowl, add the mixed herbs and rub in the fats until the mixture resembles fine crumbs. Add enough cold water to make a stiff dough. Knead it lightly then roll out the pastry, and use it to line an 18-cm (7-in) plain flan ring or sandwich cake tin.

If you are using dried onion, soak it in a little hot water for 10 minutes, then drain. Heat the oil and fry the fresh onion until tender; drain it. Put the fresh or dried onion into the pastry case with the cheese and sprinkle over the chives. Beat together the eggs, milk and seasoning. Spoon over the onion filling. Bake towards the top of the oven at 200°C

(400°F) mark 6 for about 30–40 minutes, until golden.

Herb and mushroom burgers with spicy tomato sauce

450 g (1 lb) lean minced beef, chuck or blade
10 ml (2 level tsps) dried minced onion or 1 small onion, skinned and grated
50 g (2 oz) mushrooms, wiped and roughly chopped
5 ml (1 level tsp) dried mixed herbs
salt and pepper
melted butter or oil for cooking

For spicy tomato sauce
298-g (10-oz) can tomato soup
10 ml (2 level tsps) dried minced onion or 1 small onion, skinned and finely grated
5 ml (1 level tsp) horseradish sauce
large pinch of salt
pinch of pepper
1·25 ml ($\frac{1}{4}$ level tsp) chili seasoning
pinch of garlic salt
dash of Worcestershire sauce
squeeze of lemon juice
5 ml (1 tsp) vinegar

Serves 4

Combine all the sauce ingredients in a pan, bring to the boil, cover and simmer gently for 20 minutes. Meanwhile prepare the burgers – combine all the rest of the ingredients except the fat, mix well and shape into 8 round cakes. To cook, brush sparingly with melted butter or oil, and grill for 4–6 minutes turning once, or fry in a little fat in a frying pan, turning once and allowing the same amount of time. Serve the burgers coated in sauce or serve the sauce separately. Serve with buttered noodles.

Bacon and egg pie

350 g (12 oz) streaky bacon rashers, rinded
15 ml (1 tbsp) oil
45 ml (3 level tbsps) flour
200 ml (7 fl oz) chicken stock
2·5 ml ($\frac{1}{2}$ level tsp) dried marjoram or 7·5 ml (1$\frac{1}{2}$ tsps) chopped fresh marjoram
pinch of nutmeg
15 ml (1 level tbsp) dried sweet pepper flakes
198-g (7-oz) can sweetcorn kernels, drained
salt and pepper
210-g (7$\frac{1}{2}$-oz) pkt frozen puff pastry, thawed
2 hardboiled eggs, shelled and halved
milk for glazing

Serves 4

Chop the bacon roughly, put it in a pan and fry gently in oil for 5–10 minutes – do not allow it to turn golden. Remove it from the pan and drain off all but 15 ml (1 tbsp) of the fat. Add the flour to the fat remaining in the pan. Cook it gently for 2 minutes, remove from the heat and stir in the stock gradually. Return the pan to the heat, bring it to the boil, stirring, and cook for 2 minutes. Stir in the marjoram, nutmeg and sweet pepper flakes. Add the bacon and sweetcorn. Season to taste then leave the mixture to cool.

Roll out half the pastry and use it to line a 20·5-cm (8-in) pie plate. Spoon in the sauce and press the eggs into the surface. Cover with remaining pastry. Press the edges to seal, trim and decorate. Brush the pie with a little milk and bake in the oven at 200 C (400 F) mark 6 for 35–40 minutes until golden. Serve hot or cold.

Cannelloni

175 g (6 oz) cannelloni
15 ml (1 tbsp) dried onion flakes or 1 medium onion, skinned and chopped
30 ml (2 tbsps) oil
25 g (1 oz) butter
225 g (8 oz) mushrooms, wiped and chopped
350 g (12 oz) cooked ham or bacon, diced
50 g (2 oz) Cheddar cheese, grated
5 ml (1 level tsp) Italian seasoning
salt and pepper
pinch garlic salt

For cheese sauce
400 ml ($\frac{3}{4}$ pt) milk
1 bayleaf
blade of mace
6 peppercorns
15 ml (1 tbsp) dried onion flakes or 1 medium onion, skinned and chopped
40 g (1$\frac{1}{2}$ oz) butter
60 ml (4 level tbsps) flour
175 g (6 oz) Cheddar cheese, grated
salt
nutmeg
Parmesan cheese

Serves 3–4

Boil the cannelloni as instructed on the packet then drain. If you are using onion flakes for filling, cover them with warm water and leave for 10 minutes, then drain. Heat the oil and butter in a pan, fry the onion and mushrooms until cooked, add the ham and mix well. Cool. Add the cheese, Italian seasoning, salt, pepper and garlic salt. Stuff the cannelloni with the ham mixture and arrange them in a buttered shallow ovenproof dish.

To prepare the sauce, bring the milk to the boil with the bayleaf, mace, peppercorns and onion. Cover and leave for 10 minutes, then strain it. Melt the butter in a pan, stir in the flour and cook gently for 2 minutes. Remove it from the heat and gradually stir in the milk. Bring to the boil, stirring, and cook for 2 minutes. Stir in the cheese and add salt and nutmeg to taste. Pour the sauce over the cannelloni. Sprinkle generously with grated Parmesan cheese. Bake at 180°C (350°F) mark 4 for 30 minutes, or until golden.

Chicken flan with peppers and mace

150 g (5 oz) plain flour
pinch of salt
2·5 ml ($\frac{1}{2}$ level tsp) mixed dried herbs
75 g (3 oz) fat, half butter or margarine and half lard

For filling

15 ml (1 tbsp) dried sweet pepper flakes or $\frac{1}{2}$ small red pepper, seeded and sliced
15 ml (1 tbsp) oil
100 g (4 oz) cooked chicken, diced
2 large eggs
150 ml ($\frac{1}{4}$ pt) milk
1·25 ml ($\frac{1}{4}$ level tsp) ground mace
salt and pepper
30 ml (2 level tbsps) Parmesan cheese, grated

Serves 4

Prepare the flan case as for savoury cheese flan, see page 102. If you are using dried pepper, soak it for 10 minutes, then drain. Fry the fresh pepper. Place it in the pastry case with the chicken. Beat together the eggs, milk, mace and seasoning. Spoon this

over the chicken mixture and sprinkle with cheese. Bake as for savoury cheese flan.

Noodles rusticana

4 small onions
225 g (8 oz) back bacon rashers, rinded
100 g (4 oz) butter
225 g (8 oz) noodle nests
50 g (2 oz) Parmesan cheese, grated
10 ml (2 level tsps) dried parsley or 30 ml (2 tbsps) chopped fresh parsley
10 ml (2 level tsps) mixed dried herbs
ground pepper
175 g (6 oz) mature Cheddar cheese, grated
extra chopped parsley for garnish

For tomato sauce

10 ml (2 level tsps) dried minced onion or onion flakes or 1 small onion, skinned and finely chopped
2 rashers of bacon, rinded and chopped
knob of butter
20 ml (1$\frac{1}{2}$ level tbsps) flour
425-g (15-oz) can tomatoes
1 clove
$\frac{1}{2}$ bayleaf
5 ml (1 level tsp) dried rosemary or 15 ml (1 tbsp) chopped fresh rosemary, or 5 ml (1 level tsp) dried mixed herbs
salt and pepper

Serves 4

First prepare the tomato sauce. Fry the fresh onion and bacon in the butter for 5 minutes. Stir in the flour and gradually add the tomatoes with their juice, also the dried onion, if used, clove, herbs seasoning. Simmer gently for 15 minutes, then sieve and if necessary re-season. Meanwhile skin the whole onions and parboil them in salted water for about 5 minutes, then drain them and cut in half. Cut the bacon into small pieces, gently fry it in its own fat until cooked then remove to one side. Melt 25 g (1 oz) butter and fry the onion halves until golden brown, turning them carefully to retain their shape – keep them warm. Cook the noodles in fast boiling water for 3–4 minutes, then drain well. Melt the remaining butter and add the noodles, bacon, Parmesan cheese, parsley, mixed herbs and pepper. Toss lightly to combine the ingredients and pile them into a heated shallow serving dish. Garnish with onion halves and sprinkle with more parsley. Serve with a bowl of grated Cheddar cheese, and the hot tomato sauce.

* Frankfurters garnis

2 210-g (2 7½-oz) pkt frankfurters
30 ml (2 tbsps) dried onion flakes or 1 medium onion, skinned and chopped
425-g (15-oz) can tomatoes
30 ml (2 tbsps) sherry
2·5 ml (½ level tsp) dried thyme or 7·5 ml (1½ tsps) chopped fresh thyme
2 bayleaves
salt
ground pepper
chopped parsley for garnish

Serves 4

Cut the frankfurters into chunky slices. Put them in a casserole. Put the onions in cold water, bring to the boil, remove from the heat and drain well. Add them to the frankfurters.

Combine the tomatoes and juice with the sherry. Pour them over the casserole and add all the herbs and seasonings. Cover and bake in the oven at 180°C (350°F) mark 4 for about 1 hour. Half-way through the cooking time stir the contents of the casserole. Before serving,

remove the bayleaves. Garnish with chopped parsley.

Fish cakes

450 g (1 lb) old potatoes, peeled
25 g (1 oz) butter or margarine
225 g (8 oz) cooked or canned fish e.g. salmon, tuna, smoked haddock or cod
5 ml (1 tsp) lemon juice
1·25 ml (¼ level tsp) garlic salt
pinch black pepper
pinch ground mace
2·5 ml (½ level tsp) dried chives or 7·5 ml (1½ tsps) chopped fresh chives
2·5 ml (½ level tsp) dried thyme or 7·5 ml (1½ tsps) chopped fresh thyme
1 large egg, beaten
50 g (2 oz) fresh white breadcrumbs
cooking oil

Serves 4

Cook the potatoes in boiling salted water until tender, then drain them. Mash the potatoes with the butter, fish, lemon juice, seasonings and herbs. Leave the mixture to cool then shape it into 8 cakes. Coat the fish cakes with beaten egg and breadcrumbs.

Deep or shallow fry in oil until golden on both sides. Drain on kitchen paper and serve at once with chive sauce.

Chive sauce

50 g (2 oz) butter
15 ml (1 level tbsp) French mustard
15 ml (1 tbsp) vinegar
pinch of salt and pepper
2 egg yolks
10 ml (2 level tsps) dried chives or 30 ml (2 tbsps) chopped fresh chives

Heat the butter gently, until almost melted, then remove the pan from the heat. Mix together the mustard, vinegar, salt, pepper and egg yolks. Gradually whisk the egg yolk mixture into the butter and add the chives. (If you are using dried chives prepare the sauce at least $\frac{1}{2}$ hour before required to allow the flavour to mature.) Serve the sauce cold, or warm it carefully over a pan of hot water.

Chicken turnovers

15 ml (1 tbsp) dried onion flakes or 1 medium onion, skinned and chopped
100 g (4 oz) streaky bacon rashers, rinded
5 ml (1 level tsp) dried parsley or 15 ml (1 tbsp) chopped fresh parsley
5 ml (1 level tsp) cornflour
5 ml (1 level tsp) dried mixed herbs
60 ml (4 tbsps) water or chicken stock
225 g (8 oz) cooked chicken, roughly chopped
pinch ground mace
pinch celery salt
210-g (7$\frac{1}{2}$-oz) pkt frozen puff pastry, thawed
beaten egg to glaze

Serves 4

If you are using dried onion, soak it in warm water for 10 minutes, then drain. Scissor-snip the bacon, put it in a pan with the fresh onion and cook until the onion is soft. Stir in the parsley, cornflour, mixed herbs and dried onion if you are using it. Cook for 1–2 minutes. Add water or stock to the pan and cook, stirring, until thickened. Stir the chopped chicken into the sauce and add the mace, celery salt and pepper to taste.

Roll out the pastry into a 30-cm (12-in) square and cut into four 15-cm (6-in) squares. Divide the mixture between the squares, moisten the edges, fold them in half and seal. Brush the turnovers with a little beaten egg and

place them on a baking sheet. Bake at 200°C (400°F) mark 6 for 20–30 minutes until golden. Serve hot or cold.

* Zesty haddock

700 g (1$\frac{1}{2}$ lb) fresh or frozen haddock fillet
salt and pepper
150 ml ($\frac{1}{4}$ pt) soured cream
1·25 ml ($\frac{1}{4}$ level tsp) dry mustard
1·25 ml ($\frac{1}{4}$ level tsp) ground ginger
2·5 ml ($\frac{1}{2}$ level tsp) dried thyme or 7·5 ml (1$\frac{1}{2}$ tsps) chopped fresh thyme
paprika
chopped fresh parsley to garnish

Serves 4

Divide the haddock into 4 serving portions and place them in a lightly greased shallow baking dish. Season with salt and pepper. Mix together the cream, mustard, ginger and thyme and spread over the fish. Bake in the oven at 180°C (350°F) mark 4 for 20–25 minutes. Serve immediately, topped with paprika and parsley.

Chicken rice sauté

30 ml (2 tbsps) dried onion flakes or 1 medium onion, skinned
100 g (4 oz) long grain rice
salt and ground pepper
$\frac{1}{2}$ red pepper, seeded
225 g (8 oz) lean bacon rashers, rinded
50 g (2 oz) butter
175 g (6 oz) cooking apples
225 g (8 oz) cooked chicken, chopped
2·5 ml ($\frac{1}{2}$ level tsp) dried tarragon or 7·5 ml (1$\frac{1}{2}$ tsps) chopped fresh tarragon

Serves 4

Soak the onion flakes in warm water for 10 minutes, then drain them. Cook the rice in boiling salted water for 10–12 minutes, then drain it. Chop the fresh onion, slice the pepper and snip the bacon finely. Melt the butter in a large pan and sauté the onion, pepper and bacon until the onion is soft. Peel, core and chop the apples and add them to the onion mixture with the rice, chicken, herbs, salt and pepper. Heat gently for 15 minutes. Serve with a sliced tomato salad.

Individual pizza

30 ml (2 tbsps) dried onion flakes or 1 large onion, skinned and chopped
225 g (8 oz) self raising flour
5 ml (1 level tsp) salt
about 150 ml ($\frac{1}{4}$ pt) cooking oil
water
40 g (1$\frac{1}{2}$ oz) butter
5 ml (1 level tsp) dried oregano
175 g (6 oz) sliced salami
4 tomatoes, sliced
175g (6 oz) cooking cheese, grated

Serves 4

Soak the onion flakes in a little boiling water for 10 minutes then drain them. Mix the flour and salt together in a basin. Stir in 30 ml (2 tbsps) oil and sufficient water to mix to a fairly soft dough. Divide the dough into four and roll out into thin rounds. Fry one at a time on each side in the remaining oil, until golden brown. Drain on absorbent paper.

Melt the butter in a saucepan and sauté the onion (fresh or dried) until transparent. Stir in the oregano. Divide the onion between the pizza. Top each with quartered slices of salami, tomato slices and grated cheese. Place them on a baking sheet and cook in the oven at 190°C (375°F) mark 5 for about 20 minutes.

Bacon burgers with parsley sauce

15 ml (1 level tbsp) dried minced onion or 1 medium onion, skinned
350 g (12 oz) lean bacon, rinded
105 ml (7 level tbsps) fresh white bread-crumbs
1·25 ml ($\frac{1}{4}$ level tsp) dry mustard
1·25 ($\frac{1}{4}$ level tsp) ground nutmeg
freshly ground black pepper
beaten egg
fat for frying

For sauce
25 g (1 oz) butter
45 ml (3 level tbsps) flour
300 ml ($\frac{1}{2}$ pt) milk or stock
10 ml (2 level tsps) dried parsley or 30 ml (2 tbsps) chopped fresh parsley
5 ml (1 tsp) lemon juice, optional
salt and pepper

Serves 4

Soak the dried minced onion in 20 ml (1$\frac{1}{2}$ tbsps) water for 10 minutes. Mince the bacon and fresh onion finely and combine it with the breadcrumbs, mustard, nutmeg, dried onion if used and a good turn of pepper from the mill. Add enough egg to make the mixture bind together. Turn it on to a floured board and shape into 8 cakes. Shallow fry in the hot fat for 6–7 minutes, turning the cakes 2–3 times with a fork and spoon, until they are cooked through and golden.

Meanwhile prepare the sauce. Melt the butter in a pan, stir in the flour and cook over low heat for 2 minutes. Remove the pan from the heat and gradually stir in the milk or stock. Return it to the heat and bring to the boil, stirring. Add the parsley and cook gently for 5 minutes. Stir in the lemon juice and seasoning to taste. Serve the burgers with sauce.

Sausage and apple braise

450 g (1 lb) cooking apples, peeled and cored
450 g (1 lb) leeks, trimmed
450 g (1 lb) pork sausage meat
63-g (2¼-oz) pkt instant potato
salt and freshly ground pepper
200 ml (7 fl oz) dry cider
5 ml (1 level tsp) dried mixed herbs
chopped fresh parsley or mint for garnish

Serves 4

Cut the apples into thick, even slices. Finely slice the leeks and wash them well. Put the apples in boiling water, bring back to the boil and blanch for 1 minute. Drain and cool quickly. Repeat this with the leeks.

With wetted hands, shape the sausage meat into balls about the size of a large cherry. In a lightly buttered, 1·7-l (3-pt) ovenproof dish layer up the apple, leek and half the sausage balls with a sprinkling of instant potato and seasoning between layers. Finish with the remaining sausage balls, as a topping. Mix the cider with herbs and pour it over the sausage ball mixture. Bake at 190°C (375°F) mark 5 for about 1 hour. Serve sprinkled with chopped parsley or mint. *Note* Frozen, blanched, unsweetened apple slices are equally suitable.

Lasagne al forno

2 396-g (14-oz) cans tomatoes
63-g (2¼-oz) can tomato paste
2·5 ml (½ level tsp) dried marjoram or 7·5 ml (1½ tsps) chopped fresh marjoram
2·5 ml (½ level tsp) dried oregano
salt and pepper
5 ml (1 level tsp) sugar
225 g (8 oz) cooked veal or ham, diced
100 g (4 oz) lasagne
175 g (6 oz) Ricotta or cream cheese
50 g (2 oz) Parmesan cheese, grated
225 g (8 oz) Mozarella cheese, sliced

Serves 4

Combined the canned tomatoes with their juice, the tomato paste, marjoram, oregano, seasonings and sugar; simmer gently uncovered for about 30 minutes then add the veal or ham. Cook the lasagne in boiling salted water for about 10–15 minutes (or as stated on the packet) and drain well.

Cover the base of a fairly deep ovenproof dish with a layer of the tomato and meat sauce. Add half the lasagne, put in another layer of the sauce, then cover with the cheeses, using half of each kind. Repeat these layers with the remaining ingredients, finishing with a layer of cheese. Bake in the oven at 190°C (375°F) mark 5, for about 30 minutes, until golden and bubbling on top. Serve at once.

Vegetable Dishes

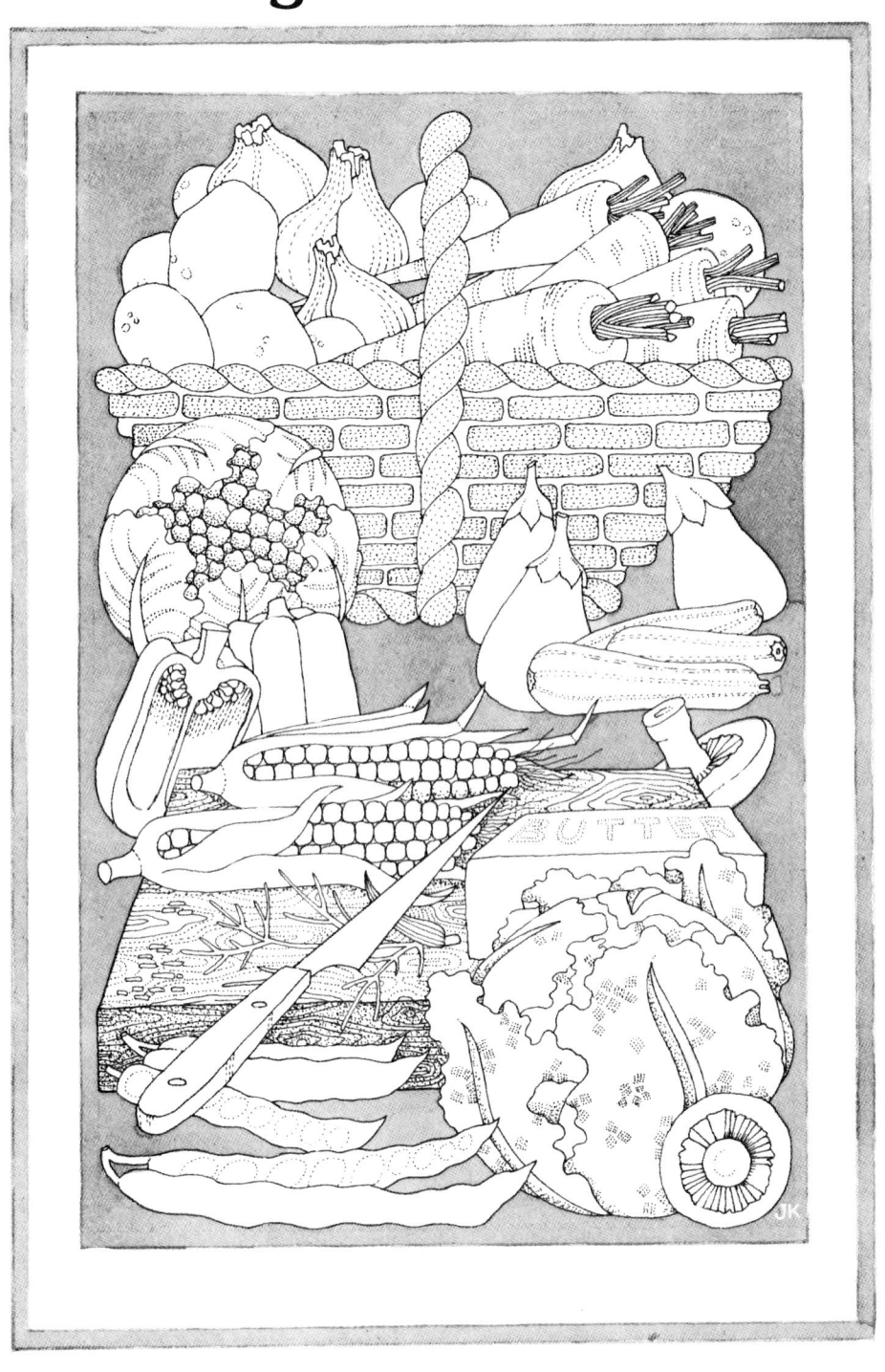

Spicy cauliflower

1 large egg
salt
freshly ground black pepper
450 g (1 lb) cauliflower florets
browned breadcrumbs
deep oil for frying

For sauce
90 ml (6 tbsps) oil
90 ml (6 tbsps) vinegar
2·5 ml ($\frac{1}{2}$ level tsp) paprika
2·5 ml ($\frac{1}{2}$ level tsp) garlic granules or 2
   cloves garlic, skinned and crushed
chopped parsley for garnish

Serves 4

Beat the egg lightly with the seasoning. Dip the florets into the egg, then into breadcrumbs and coat thoroughly. Heat the oil to 190°C (375°F) and deep fry the coated florets for 5–7 minutes until golden brown. Drain them on kitchen paper and keep them warm. Meanwhile, have ready the sauce ingredients in a small pan. Bring them to the boil, simmer for 1 minute and pour the sauce over the crisp florets. Garnish with chopped parsley and serve at once.

Oriental carrots

1 kg (2$\frac{1}{4}$ lb) carrots, pared
5 ml (1 level tsp) caster sugar
25 g (1 oz) butter
1·25 ml ($\frac{1}{4}$ level tsp) dried minced garlic
   or 1 clove garlic, skinned and crushed
90 ml (6 tbsps) water
30 ml (2 tbsps) white wine vinegar
2·5 ml ($\frac{1}{2}$ level tsp) salt
2·5 ml ($\frac{1}{2}$ level tsp) whole cumin seed
1·25 ml ($\frac{1}{4}$ level tsp) paprika
ground pepper
chopped parsley

Serves 4–6

Cut the carrots into thick matchsticks. Place them in a saucepan and add the sugar, butter and garlic. Combine the water, vinegar, salt, cumin, paprika and the pepper and pour over the vegetables. Bring to the boil, then reduce the heat to a simmer. Cover with a lid and cook for about 20 minutes if a crunchy texture is preferred, or cook for a further 7 minutes until tender. Stir with a wooden spoon occasionally to prevent the carrots sticking to pan. Serve garnished with chopped parsley.

Carrots with dill cream sauce

450 g (1 lb) carrots, peeled and sliced
2·5 ml ($\frac{1}{2}$ level tsp) dried dill weed or
   7·5 ml (1$\frac{1}{2}$ tsps) fresh chopped dill
150 ml ($\frac{1}{4}$ pt) milk
seasoned salt
pepper
15 ml (1 level tbsp) cornflour
60–70 ml (4–5 tbsps) single cream
chopped fresh parsley or dill for garnish

Serves 4

Put the carrots into an ovenproof dish. Mix together the dill, milk and seasoning and pour over the carrots. Cover tightly. Bake in the oven at 200°C (400°F) mark 6 for about 30 minutes or until the carrots are tender. Strain the liquid into a saucepan. Blend the cornflour with a little cold water and stir into the milk. Bring to the boil, stirring continuously. Add the cream and heat gently but do not boil. Adjust the seasoning. Stir in the carrots. Put in a warm serving dish and sprinkle with chopped parsley or dill.

Sunshine carrots

450 g (1 lb) young carrots, washed
15 ml (1 level tbsp) soft brown sugar
5 ml (1 level tsp) cornflour
1·25 ml ($\frac{1}{4}$ level tsp) salt
1·25 ml ($\frac{1}{4}$ level tsp) ground ginger
150 ml ($\frac{1}{4}$ pt) unsweetened orange juice
25 g (1 oz) butter
chopped parsley for garnish

Serves 4

Cook the carrots in boiling salted water until just tender then drain them well. Meanwhile combine the sugar, cornflour, salt and ginger in a small saucepan. Blend in the orange juice and bring to the boil, stirring constantly until the mixture thickens and bubbles. Stir in the butter and when it has completely melted, pour the sauce over the carrots, tossing to coat them evenly. Garnish with the chopped parsley. Serve with pork, gammon or bacon.

* Whole bean provençale

175 g (6 oz) onions, skinned and tinly sliced
45 ml (3 tbsps) cooking oil
1·25 ml ($\frac{1}{4}$ level tsp) garlic granules or 1 clove garlic, skinned and crushed
396-ml (14-oz) can tomatoes, drained
450 g (1 lb) frozen whole green beans
5 ml (1 level tsp) dried basil or 15 ml (1 tbsp) chopped fresh basil
salt
freshly ground black pepper

Serves 4

Sauté the onions in the oil until soft but not brown. Add the garlic and tomatoes, then the frozen beans, basil, salt and pepper. Cover and simmer gently until the beans are cooked, about 10 minutes.

Alternatively cook in the oven at 180°C (350°F) mark 4 for about 30 minutes. Serve with roast lamb.

Broad beans with poppy seeds

450 g (1 lb) shelled broad beans
25 g (1 oz) butter
1 small onion, skinned and chopped
2–3 rashers streaky bacon, rinded and chopped
salt
freshly ground black pepper
poppy seeds

Serves 4

Cook the beans in boiling salted water until tender, then drain them well. Melt the butter in a saucepan, add the chopped onion and cook until it is soft but not brown. Add the bacon and cook until crisp. Add the beans, season with salt and pepper then toss over a low heat for a few minutes. Serve sprinkled liberally with poppy seeds.

Foil baked corn on the cob

4 frozen corn cobs
50 g (2 oz) butter
5 ml (1 level tsp) dried chervil or tarragon or 15 ml (1 tbsp) chopped fresh chervil or tarragon
salt
freshly ground black pepper

Serves 4

Cook the corn in boiling salted water for 5 minutes. Drain and place each cob in the centre of a piece of buttered foil. Melt the butter, add the herb and use to brush over the corn. Wrap the foil around the corn, making a double fold along the top and at each end to seal the butter in. Put the packages on a baking sheet and cook in the oven at 170°C (325°F) mark 3 for 10 minutes. Serve in the foil, seasoned with salt and pepper.

*Courgettes and tomatoes au gratin

450 g (1 lb) courgettes
25 g (1 oz) butter
15 ml (1 tbsp) oil
salt and freshly ground pepper
425-g (15-oz) can tomatoes, drained
1·25 ml ($\frac{1}{4}$ level tsp) celery salt
1·25 ml ($\frac{1}{4}$ level tsp) onion salt
5–10 ml (1–2 level tsps) dried oregano
3 tomatoes, skinned
5 ml (1 level tsp) dry mustard
5 ml (1 tsp) water
150 ml (5 fl oz) natural yoghurt
175 g (6 oz) grated Cheddar cheese
1 egg yolk

Serves 4

Trim the courgettes and cut them into slices 0·5 cm ($\frac{1}{4}$ in) thick. Melt the butter with the oil and sauté the courgettes gently until just tender – 10–15 minutes; season well and keep them warm. Put the canned tomatoes in a saucepan with the celery salt, onion salt and oregano. Boil them rapidly, uncovered, to give a thick pulp. Halve the fresh tomatoes, discard the seeds and chop them roughly; add to the tomato pulp. Cream the mustard with the water. Put the yoghurt, 75 g (3 oz) of the cheese, egg yolk and mustard in a saucepan. Beat them together, then cook gently, stirring until the mixture thickens. Arrange the courgettes in the base of a warm 900-ml (1$\frac{1}{2}$-pt) ovenproof dish. Sprinkle the remaining cheese over and season well with salt and pepper. Spoon the

really hot tomato mixture over and spread it evenly. Carefully pour the yoghurt sauce over the tomatoes. Place the dish under a hot grill to heat through and brown the topping. Serve immediately.

Baked courgettes with cream and almonds

450 g (1 lb) courgettes
25 g (1 oz) butter
2·5 ml ($\frac{1}{2}$ level tsp) ground mace
salt and pepper
113-ml (4-fl oz) carton double cream
45 ml (3 level tbsps) flaked almonds, toasted

Serves 4

Trim the courgettes and cut into 1-cm ($\frac{1}{2}$-in) slices. Melt the butter and toss in the courgettes with the mace and a good seasoning of salt and pepper. Bake in a shallow ovenproof dish at 190°C (375°F) mark 5 for 25-30 minutes, or until tender and golden, turning occasionally. Pour the cream over and sprinkle with toasted almonds. Serve immediately.

Casseroled potatoes with parsnips

450 g (1 lb) potatoes
450 g (1 lb) parsnips
knob of butter
7·5 ml (1$\frac{1}{2}$ level tsps) seasoning salt
freshly ground black pepper
150 ml ($\frac{1}{4}$ pt) stock
2·5 ml ($\frac{1}{2}$ level tsp) dried rosemary or 7·5 ml (1$\frac{1}{2}$ tsps) chopped fresh rosemary

Serves 6

Peel and slice the potatoes and parsnips evenly. Butter a 1·7-l (3-pt) ovenproof dish with a lid. Layer the sliced potatoes and parsnips in this, sprinkling seasoning salt and pepper between the layers. Bring the stock to the boil with the rosemary, pour it over the vegetables. Cover with a lid and bake at 190°C (375°F) mark 5 for about 1 hour, or until tender.

Potatoes creole-style

knob of butter
700 g (1½ lb) potatoes
1 large green pepper, seeded and finely sliced
1 large onion, skinned and finely sliced
3 large firm tomatoes, skinned and chopped
2·5 ml (½ level tsp) dried rosemary or 7·5 ml (1½ tsps) fresh chopped rosemary
2·5 ml (½ level tsp) paprika
salt
30 ml (2 tbsps) stock or water
chopped fresh parsley

Serves 4–6

Butter a 1·7-l (3-pt) ovenproof dish. Peel and thinly slice the potatoes. Layer them in the buttered dish with the pepper, onion and tomatoes. Sprinkle rosemary, paprika and salt liberally between each layer, pour over the stock, cover and bake at 190°C (375°F) mark 5 for about 1 hour or until tender. Serve sprinkled with chopped parsley.

Golden sauté potatoes

1 kg (2¼ lb) potatoes
5 ml (1 level tsp) fenugreek seeds, crushed
2·5 ml (½ level tsp) turmeric
1·25 ml (¼ level tsp) cayenne pepper
pinch of salt
50 g (2 oz) butter

Serves 6

Peel the potatoes and cut them into 2-cm (¾-in) dice. Mix together the spices and salt. Sprinkle the mixture evenly over the potatoes and toss. Melt the butter in a large heavy frying pan. Add the spiced potatoes and sauté gently for 15–20 minutes, turning occasionally, until crisp and golden.

Ratatouille layered pudding

50 g (2 oz) butter
225 g (8 oz) aubergines, sliced
150 g (5 oz) leeks, sliced and washed
100 g (4 oz) green pepper, seeded and sliced
15 ml (1 tbsp) dried onion flakes
2 whole caps canned red pimiento, sliced
2·5 ml (½ level tsp) garlic salt
1·25 ml (¼ level tsp) cayenne pepper
5 ml (1 level tsp) Italian seasoning
200 g (7 oz) self raising flour
100 g (3½ oz) shredded suet
salt and pepper
about 120 ml (7 tbsps) water
175 g (6 oz) red Leicester cheese, grated

Serves 6

Grease a 1·4-l (2½-pt) pudding basin. Place a circle of non-stick paper in the base. Melt the butter in a large frying pan. Sauté the aubergine, leek and pepper for about 5 minutes. Meanwhile soak the onion flakes in a little hot water for about 10 minutes and drain. Add the reconstituted onion flakes, sliced pimiento, garlic salt and cayenne pepper to the aubergine mixture. Stir in 2·5 ml (½ level tsp) Italian seasoning.

Sift the flour into a basin, add the suet, remaining Italian seasoning, salt and pepper. Mix to a soft dough with the water. Divide the pastry into three; roll each piece out to a circle, graduating in size. Place one circle at the base of the basin. Spoon half the vegetable mixture over it. Sprinkle with half the cheese. Repeat the layering once and finish with a circle of pastry. Cover with greased kitchen foil and steam for 3 hours.

Peperoni ripieni

salt
225 g (8 oz) aubergines, diced
3 large green peppers
3 large red peppers
30 ml (2 tbsps) oil
50 g (2 oz) butter
100 g (4 oz) onion, skinned and sliced
1·25 ml ($\frac{1}{4}$ level tsp) dried minced garlic or 1 large clove garlic, skinned and crushed
350 g (12 oz) courgettes, trimmed and sliced
225 g (8 oz) tomatoes, quartered
75 ml (5 tbsps) white wine
1·25 ml ($\frac{1}{4}$ level tsp) ground bayleaves
ground pepper
chopped parsley

Serves 6

Sprinkle 10 ml (2 level tsps) salt over the aubergine and leave for about 30 minutes. Rinse and pat dry. From the stem end of the peppers cut a lid 2 cm ($\frac{3}{4}$ in) down. Scoop out the membrane and seeds. Place the pepper shells and lids in boiling water, bring it back to the boil and blanch for 2 minutes. Drain and cool the peppers and arrange them in a lightly oiled ovenproof dish. Heat the oil and butter, add the onion and sauté for 2–3 minutes. Stir in the garlic, courgettes, tomatoes, aubergines, 45 ml

(3 tbsps) wine and the ground bayleaves. Season well with salt and pepper. Cook until the vegetables are soft but not 'mushy' and the liquid is absorbed. Stir the vegetables often during cooking to prevent them sticking to the pan.

Divide the filling between the peppers, and replace the lids. Spoon the remaining wine into the base of the dish. Bake uncovered at 190°C (375°F) mark 5 for about 30 minutes. Allow to cool in the dish. Remove the lids, spoon the juices over the pepper filling. Add a little chopped parsley and replace the lids.

Aubergines au gratin

2 medium sized aubergines
salt
knob of butter
1 small onion, skinned and finely chopped
396-g (14-oz) can tomatoes, drained
5 ml (1 level tsp) dried oregano
freshly ground black pepper
6 rashers back bacon, rinded and cut into large pieces
cooking oil
600 ml (1 pt) cheese sauce

Serves 4

Wash, dry and thinly slice the aubergines. Spread the slices out on a large tray or plate, sprinkle with salt and leave for 1 hour to extract the bitter juices. Melt the butter and sauté the onion until transparent. Add the tomatoes and oregano, with salt and pepper to season. Simmer gently for 10 minutes. Put the bacon in a frying pan without fat and heat gently until the fat runs, then fry until crisp. Dry the aubergines with absorbent paper.

Heat 45 ml (3 tbsps) oil in a pan and

sauté the aubergines a few slices at a time until brown on both sides. Place half the aubergines in the base of a deep ovenproof dish and spoon the tomato mixture evenly over. Scatter the bacon over the tomato. Top with the remaining sliced aubergines, and pour the cheese sauce over. Bake in the oven at 190°C (375°F) mark 5 for about 30 minutes, until golden brown.

Curried rice with spinach

25 g (1 oz) butter
1 medium onion, skinned and chopped
10–15 ml (2–3 level tsps) curry powder
225 g (8 oz) long grain rice
600 ml (1 pt) stock
salt
100 g (4 oz) spinach

Serves 4–6

Melt the butter in a heavy pan and fry the onion with the curry powder for 2–3 minutes. Stir in the rice then add the stock and salt to taste. Simmer gently, covered, for 10 minutes, stirring occasionally. Meanwhile, wash and trim the spinach, discarding any thick stems. Shred it coarsely with a sharp knife then stir it into the rice and simmer, covered, for 5–8 minutes, adding more stock if necessary. Serve as an accompaniment to grilled meats.

Cabbage with caraway

1 small white cabbage
5 ml (1 level tsp) caraway seeds
2·5 ml ($\frac{1}{2}$ level tsp) ground nutmeg
2·5 ml ($\frac{1}{2}$ level tsp) onion salt
200 ml ($\frac{1}{3}$ pt) chicken stock
knob of butter

Serves 4–6

Wash and dry the cabbage. Cut it in half and discard the thick stem. Shred the cabbage with a sharp knife and put it in a heavy saucepan with the remaining ingredients. Bring to the boil, then reduce the heat and simmer gently, covered, for 10–15 minutes, until tender.

Sweet and sour red cabbage

1 medium sized red cabbage
1 small onion, skinned and finely chopped
50 g (2 oz) butter
30 ml (2 level tbsps) demerara sugar
15 ml (1 level tbsp) flour
2·5 ml ($\frac{1}{2}$ level tsp) ground allspice
5 ml (1 level tsp) salt
60 ml (4 tbsps) malt vinegar
300 ml ($\frac{1}{2}$ pt) water
10 ml (2 tsps) Worcestershire sauce

Serves 6

Trim the cabbage, remove the coarse stem and shred the leaves finely. Put it in a saucepan with the remaining ingredients. Cover the pan and cook gently on top of the cooker, stirring occasionally, for about 20 minutes or until tender.

Buttered swede

1 kg (2$\frac{1}{4}$ lb) swede
25 g (1 oz) butter
45 ml (3 tbsps) stock
2·5 ml ($\frac{1}{2}$ level tsp) ground nutmeg
1·25 ml ($\frac{1}{4}$ level tsp) barbecue seasoning
salt and pepper

Serves 6

Peel the swede and cut it into 2-cm ($\frac{3}{4}$-in) cubes. Melt the butter and sauté the swede, turning frequently, for about 5 minutes. Add the stock, nutmeg, barbecue seasoning and salt and pepper. Cover and cook gently, stirring occasionally, for about 20 minutes, or until tender.

Baked onions with sage

450 g (1 lb) small onions
60 ml (4 tbsps) water
15 ml (1 level tbsp) granulated sugar
2·5 ml ($\frac{1}{2}$ level tsp) dried sage or
 7·5 ml (1$\frac{1}{2}$ tsps) fresh chopped sage
salt and pepper
Serves 4

Skin the onions and leave them whole. Place them in a shallow casserole. Spoon the water over and sprinkle with the sugar and sage. Season with salt and pepper. Bake uncovered at 200°C (400°F) mark 6 for about 30 minutes or until tender and golden brown. Turn the onions over once or twice during the cooking time.

Stuffed mushrooms

12 flat mushrooms, wiped
75 g (3 oz) onion, skinned and finely chopped
knob of butter
120 ml (8 level tbsps) fresh white breadcrumbs
50 g (2 oz) cheese, grated
15 ml (1 level tbsp) dried parsley or 30 ml (2 tbsps) fresh chopped parsley
grated rind of 1 large lemon
2·5 ml ($\frac{1}{2}$ level tsp) ground mace
salt and freshly ground pepper
beaten egg to bind

Serves 6

Remove and chop the stalks from the mushrooms. Combine these with the onion and fry gently in the butter until soft but not coloured. Add the breadcrumbs, cheese, parsley, lemon rind, mace and seasonings. Bind these together with beaten egg and pile the mixture on to the mushroom caps. Place them on a lightly greased baking sheet and cover with foil. Bake in the oven at 190°C (375°F) mark 5 for 25–30 minutes. Serve these mushrooms on their own as a starter or as a vegetable accompaniment.

Gourmet mushrooms

25 g (1 oz) butter
1 carrot, pared and coarsely grated
1 small onion, skinned and finely chopped
1 small stick celery, trimmed and finely chopped
1·25 ml ($\frac{1}{4}$ level tsp) minced garlic or 1 clove garlic, skinned and crushed
450 g (1 lb) button mushrooms, wiped
10 coriander seeds, crushed
150 ml ($\frac{1}{4}$ pt) dry white wine
2·5 ml ($\frac{1}{2}$ level tsp) dried thyme or 7·5 ml (1$\frac{1}{2}$ tsps) fresh chopped thyme
2·5 ml ($\frac{1}{2}$ level tsp) dried parsley or 7·5 ml (1$\frac{1}{2}$ tsps) fresh chopped parsley
3 tomatoes, skinned and chopped
salt and freshly ground black pepper
15 ml (1 tbsp) freshly chopped parsley for garnish

Serves 4–6

Melt the butter and gently sauté the grated carrot, chopped onion, celery and garlic for about 5 minutes. Add the mushrooms, crushed coriander, wine and herbs and simmer gently, uncovered, for a further 5 minutes. Stir in the chopped tomatoes and seasoning to taste; simmer for a further 10–15 minutes, uncovered. Transfer to a serving dish, sprinkle with chopped parsley and serve hot.

Asparagus with béarnaise sauce

450 g (1 lb) fresh asparagus spears

For herb vinegar
60 ml (4 tbsps) white wine vinegar
6 peppercorns
1 bayleaf
2·5 ml ($\frac{1}{2}$ level tsp) dried tarragon or 7·5 ml (1$\frac{1}{2}$ tsps) fresh chopped tarragon
2·5 ml ($\frac{1}{2}$ level tsp) dried chervil or 7·5 ml (1$\frac{1}{2}$ tsps) fresh chopped chervil
1 shallot, skinned and chopped

For béarnaise sauce
2 egg yolks
75 g (3 oz) unsalted butter, softened
2·5 ml ($\frac{1}{2}$ level tsp) dried tarragon or 7·5 ml (1$\frac{1}{2}$ tsps) chopped fresh tarragon
2·5 ml ($\frac{1}{2}$ level tsp) dried chervil or 7·5 ml (1$\frac{1}{2}$ tsps) chopped fresh chervil
60 ml (4 tbsps) double cream, lightly whipped
salt and pepper

Serves 4

Put all the ingredients for the herb vinegar in a saucepan, leave uncovered and reduce by gently boiling to 15 ml (1 tbsp). Strain the vinegar into the top of a double saucepan. Blend the egg yolks with a knob of the softened butter, then add to the vinegar. Heat the water in the bottom of the double saucepan to simmering. With a wooden spoon, constantly stir the egg yolk mixture until it begins to thicken. Add the butter, a knob at a time, gradually increasing the heat. When all the butter is added, stir in the herbs and cream and adjust seasoning. Cover and keep warm.

Meanwhile wash and trim the asparagus, tie it in small bunches with string and cook in boiling salted water for 12–14 minutes, until just tender. Drain and remove the string and arrange the asparagus on a hot dish; pour the sauce over. Alternatively, serve the asparagus in a folded napkin and hand the sauce separately.

Artichokes with herb butter sauce

4 globe artichokes, trimmed
15 ml (1 tbsp) lemon juice
salt

For herb butter
60 ml (4 tbsps) white wine vinegar
1 shallot or small piece of onion, skinned and finely chopped
5 ml (1 level tsp) dried parsley or 15 ml (1 tbsp) chopped fresh parsley
5 ml (1 level tsp) dried *fines herbes*
175 g (6 oz) butter, clarified
pepper and salt

Serves 4

Soak the artichokes in cold water for about 30 minutes, to ensure they are thoroughly cleaned; drain well. Cook them in rapidly boiling water with the lemon juice and salt until the leaves will pull out easily – 30–50 minutes, depending on size. Drain them upside-down.

Meanwhile put the wine vinegar in a pan with the shallot and herbs. Boil rapidly until the liquid is reduced to about 15 ml (1 tbsp). Strain it and discard the flavourings. Stir the liquid into the melted butter and add salt and pepper to taste. Serve the artichokes with herb butter sauce.

Salads

Apple, raisin and walnut salad

30 ml (2 tbsps) lemon juice
2·5 ml ($\frac{1}{2}$ level tsp) apple pie spice
3 crisp, green eating apples
50 g (2 oz) seedless raisins
50 g (2 oz) walnuts, roughly chopped

Serves 3–4

Mix together the lemon juice and spice. Core the apples and slice them thinly. Toss the apple slices in the spiced lemon juice. Add the raisins and walnuts and toss well together. Serve as a side salad with pork, cooked bacon joint or chicken.

Avocado rice salad

45 ml (3 tbsps) olive oil
25 ml (1$\frac{1}{2}$ tbsps) white wine vinegar
5 ml (1 level tsp) dried marjoram or 15 ml (1 tbsp) fresh chopped marjoram
1·25 ml ($\frac{1}{4}$ level tsp) minced garlic or 1 small clove garlic, skinned and crushed
salt
freshly ground black pepper
5 ml (1 level tsp) brown sugar
30 ml (2 tbsps) lemon juice
2 ripe avocados
175 g (6 oz) long grain rice, cooked
2 tomatoes, skinned and chopped
4 eggs, hardboiled and halved

Serves 4

Put the oil, vinegar, marjoram, garlic, salt, pepper, sugar and 15 ml (1 tbsp) lemon juice into a small bowl. Mix them well together and allow to infuse for 1 hour. Halve the avocados, and remove the stones and skin. Cut one avocado into thin slices and toss in 15 ml (1 tbsp) lemon juice. Chop the other avocado and put it in a large bowl with the rice and tomatoes. Add the dressing and toss them well together. Put the salad in a serving dish and arrange sliced avocado and hardboiled eggs on top. This is a main course salad.

Bean sprout salad

100 g (4 oz) fresh bean sprouts
50 g (2 oz) onion, skinned and chopped
100 g (4 oz) cooked ham, cut in strips
5 ml (1 level tsp) dried mixed herbs
1·25 ml ($\frac{1}{4}$ level tsp) dried tarragon or 5 ml (1 tsp) fresh chopped tarragon
2·5 ml ($\frac{1}{2}$ level tsp) dry mustard
2·5 ml ($\frac{1}{2}$ level tsp) sugar
30 ml (2 tbsps) oil
10 ml (2 tsps) wine vinegar
1 lettuce, washed
chopped parsley for garnish

Serves 2–3

Wash and dry the bean sprouts. Combine them with the chopped onion and the strips of ham. Make a dressing by whisking or shaking together the herbs, mustard, sugar, oil and vinegar. Toss the bean sprouts, onion and ham lightly in the dressing. Serve on a bed of lettuce, garnished with chopped parsley.
Note When no fresh bean sprouts are available use a can, drained.

* Citrus spice salad

2 large oranges
2 grapefruits
6 whole cloves
seeds from 2 cardamom pods
225 g (8 oz) cottage cheese
1·25 ml ($\frac{1}{4}$ level tsp) ground cardamom

Serves 4

With a sharp knife, remove the peel and

all the pith from the oranges and grapefruits. Cut them into segments, discarding the membranes between – hold the fruit over a bowl to catch the juice. Put the juice in a heavy-based pan with the whole spices, bring to the boil then remove from the heat, cover and leave to infuse for about 30 minutes. Strain and if necessary reduce the juice to 30 ml (2 tbsps) by rapid boiling, uncovered. Spoon this juice over the fruit segments and chill. Mix the cottage cheese with the ground cardamom and and pile it into the centre of a shallow serving dish. Arrange the chilled fruit round the edge, and spoon the juice over. Serve immediately.

Ham and brown rice salad with fruit

15–30 ml (1–2 tbsps) lemon juice
2 bananas, skinned and sliced
1 eating apple, skinned, cored and chopped
100 g (4 oz) green grapes, washed, halved and pips removed
90 ml (6 level tbsps) mayonnaise
2.5 ml ($\frac{1}{2}$ level tsp) made mustard
1.25–2.5 ml ($\frac{1}{4}$–$\frac{1}{2}$ level tsp) chili seasoning
salt and pepper
100 g (4 oz) brown rice, cooked
175 g (6 oz) cooked ham, diced
lettuce
25 g (1 oz) shelled walnuts, chopped

Serves 4

Put the lemon juice into a bowl and add the bananas, apple and grapes. Toss them well together. Put the mayonnaise into a large bowl. Add the mustard, chilli seasoning, salt and pepper. Add the brown rice, ham and fruit and toss them lightly together. Arrange the salad on a lettuce-lined serving dish and sprinkle with the chopped walnuts. This is a main course salad.

Chicken and rice salad

1·6-kg (3$\frac{1}{2}$-lb) boiling chicken
1 small onion, skinned
4 cloves
2–3 strips of lemon rind
30 ml (2 tbsps) lemon juice
blade of mace
5 ml (1 level tsp) dried parsley or few sprigs fresh parsley
6 peppercorns
salt
100 g (4 oz) long grain rice
50 g (2 oz) sultanas
25 g (1 oz) seedless raisins
225 g (8 oz) white and black grapes, skinned and pipped
150 ml ($\frac{1}{4}$ pt) mayonnaise or rémoulade dressing
sliced tomatoes and watercress for garnish

Serves 6

Put the chicken into a large saucepan with the onion studded with cloves, lemon rind and juice, mace, parsley, peppercorns and salt. Add sufficient water to cover. Put the lid on the saucepan and simmer gently for about 3 hours or until the chicken is tender. Leave the chicken to cool then remove all skin and bones and dice the flesh. Strain the chicken stock, season it well and then use for cooking the rice. Drain the rice and leave it until cold. Mix together the chicken, rice, dried fruit and half the grapes. Stir in the mayonnaise, put the salad in a serving dish and garnish with the remaining grapes, the sliced tomatoes and watercress.

Rainbow coleslaw

225 g (8 oz) red cabbage
225 g (8 oz) white cabbage
1 large carrot, pared
½ green pepper, seeded
150 ml (5 fl oz) soured cream
30 ml (2 level tbsps) mayonnaise
15 ml (1 tbsp) lemon juice
2·5 ml (½ level tsp) caraway seeds
2·5 ml (½ level tsp) celery seeds
salt
freshly ground black pepper

Serves 4–6

Trim and finely shred the red and white cabbages. Wash and dry them well and put them in a large bowl. Grate the carrot on a coarse grater straight into the cabbage. Slice the green pepper finely and add it to the cabbage. Mix together the soured cream, mayonnaise, lemon juice, caraway seeds, celery seeds, salt and pepper. Pour this dressing over the coleslaw and mix thoroughly. Chill before serving.

Thousand islands sea-food salad

150 ml (¼ pt) thick mayonnaise
15 ml (1 tbsp) chopped stuffed olives
5 ml (1 level tsp) finely chopped onion
1 hardboiled egg, finely chopped
15 ml (1 level tbsp) finely chopped green
  pepper
5 ml (1 level tsp) dried parsley or 15 ml
  (1 tbsp) fresh chopped parsley
15 ml (1 level tbsp) tomato paste
15 ml (1 level tbsp) sesame seeds, lightly
  toasted
185-g (6½-oz) can dressed crab, drained
lemon slices to garnish

Serves 2

Mix together the mayonnaise, olives, onion, egg, pepper, parsley and tomato paste. Stir in half the sesame seeds. Toss the crab lightly in this dressing and turn it into a shallow serving dish. Sprinkle with the remaining sesame seeds and garnish with twists of lemon. This is a main course salad.

Note Canned salmon or tuna could be used as a less expensive alternative to crabmeat.

* Minted cucumber and celery

½ medium cucumber, finely diced
3–4 sticks celery, trimmed and finely
  sliced
150 ml (¼ pt) natural yoghurt
large pinch celery salt
1·25 ml (¼ level tsp) dried mint or 5 ml
  (1 tsp) fresh chopped mint
grated rind of ½ lemon
freshly ground black pepper

Serves 4

Put the cucumber and celery into a bowl. Add the yoghurt, celery salt, mint, lemon rind and pepper. Mix them well together and chill before serving.

Ham roulades vinaigrette

175 g (6 oz) long grain rice
60 ml (4 tbsps) salad oil
30 ml (2 tbsps) malt vinegar
2·5 ml (½ level tsp) dry mustard
2·5 ml (½ level tsp) turmeric
pinch of sugar
salt and ground pepper
4 tomatoes
8 medium slices of cooked ham
watercress

Serves 4

Cook the rice according to packet directions. In a screwtop jar, shake together the oil, vinegar, mustard, turmeric, sugar, salt and pepper. Pour this dressing over the drained rice whilst it is still warm and fork it through. Leave the rice to go cold. Slice the tomatoes and arrange them in a shallow oval dish. Season with salt and pepper. Divide the cooled rice mixture between the ham slices, roll them up carefully and place the rolls on the bed of sliced tomato. Place a sprig of watercress in the ends of each roll. Chill before serving.

Tuna bean salad

425-g (15-oz) can butter beans, drained
198-g (7-oz) can tuna fish, drained and the oil reserved
2 sticks celery, finely chopped
30–45 ml (2–3 tbsps) olive oil
30 ml (2 tbsps) cider vinegar
2·5 ml ($\frac{1}{2}$ level tsp) salad seasoning
1·25 ml ($\frac{1}{4}$ level tsp) onion salt
1·25 ml ($\frac{1}{4}$ level tsp) dry mustard
15 ml (1 tbsp) lemon juice
freshly ground black pepper
4 firm tomatoes, sliced

Serves 3–4

Put the butter beans, flaked tuna fish and celery into a bowl. Add 30–45 ml (2–3 tbsps) olive oil to the reserved tuna oil to make a total of 60 ml (4 tbsps). Add the vinegar, salad seasoning, onion salt, mustard, lemon juice and pepper. Mix them well together and add three quarters of the dressing to the tuna mixture. Arrange the sliced tomatoes on a serving dish and pour the remaining dressing over the tomatoes. Pile the tuna mixture in the centre and sprinkle with more salad seasoning. Chill the salad before serving.

Tossed fresh spinach salad

60 ml (4 tbsps) salad oil
30 ml (2 tbsps) white wine vinegar
2·5 ml ($\frac{1}{2}$ level tsp) dried basil or 7·5 ml (1$\frac{1}{2}$ tsps) fresh chopped basil
2·5 ml ($\frac{1}{2}$ level tsp) salad seasoning
10 ml (2 level tsps) finely grated lemon rind
100 g (4 oz) spinach
1 lettuce heart
6 radishes, trimmed and sliced
6 spring onions, trimmed and sliced

Serves 4

Put the oil and vinegar in a screw-top jar with the basil, salad seasoning and lemon rind. Shake well and leave to stand. Wash the spinach thoroughly, discarding any tough stems; then dry thoroughly. Wash and dry the lettuce. Using your fingertips, shred the spinach and lettuce into bite size pieces. Mix these with the sliced radishes and spring onions, toss the dressing through and pile into a serving dish. Serve as a side salad with grills or cold meats.

Curried potato and frankfurter salad

300 ml ($\frac{1}{2}$ pt) thick mayonnaise
10 ml (2 tsps) lemon juice
15 ml (1 tbsp) vinegar
5–10 ml (1–2 level tsps) mild curry powder
1 kg (2$\frac{1}{4}$ lb) new potatoes, scraped
salt
2 210-g (7$\frac{1}{2}$-oz) pkts frankfurters
50 g (2 oz) gherkins, chopped
25 g (1 oz) silverskin onions, chopped finely
chopped parsley

Serves 6–8

Mix the mayonnaise with the lemon juice, vinegar and curry powder. Cut the potatoes into large dice. Cook them in boiling salted water until just cooked but still firm – 8–10 minutes, then drain them and cool. Cook the frankfurters in fast-boiling water for 5 minutes. Drain and cool them. Slice each sausage diagonally into four. Chop the ends and add these to the potatoes. Lightly fold in the curried mayonnaise, gherkins and onions. Pile the salad up on a large flat plate and arrange the remaining frankfurter slices round the edges. Sprinkle some chopped parsley over to garnish.

* Marinaded cauliflower and mushrooms

For the marinade
1·25 ml ($\frac{1}{4}$ level tsp) ground black pepper
2·5 ml ($\frac{1}{2}$ level tsp) salt
2·5 ml ($\frac{1}{2}$ level tsp) Italian seasoning
1·25 ml ($\frac{1}{4}$ level tsp) dried tarragon or
  7·5 ml ($1\frac{1}{2}$ tsps) fresh chopped tarragon
large pinch onion salt
30 ml (2 tbsps) red wine vinegar
30 ml (2 tbsps) olive oil

1 small cauliflower
100 g (4 oz) button mushrooms, wiped

Serves 4

To make the marinade, put all the ingredients into a lidded container and shake well together. Leave to infuse for $\frac{1}{2}$ hour. Trim the cauliflower and divide it into tiny sprigs. Put them in a pan of cold water and bring to the boil. Drain quickly and rinse under cold water. Drain well again. Slice the mushrooms thinly. Put the cauliflower sprigs and the mushrooms into a bowl. Pour

over the marinade and leave it for 1 hour in the refrigerator; stir once or twice during this time. Serve as a side salad.

Swedish herring salad

4 fresh rollmop herrings
1 medium onion, skinned and thinly sliced
30 ml (2 tbsps) olive oil
15 ml (1 tbsp) malt vinegar
15 ml (1 tbsp) lemon juice
5 ml (1 level tsp) fish seasoning
450 g (1 lb) potatoes, peeled and diced
225 g (8 oz) cooked beetroot, skinned and diced
150 ml (5 fl oz) soured cream
1·25 ml ($\frac{1}{4}$ level tsp) ground bayleaves
5 ml (1 level tsp) dried fennel or 15 ml (1 tbsp) fresh chopped fennel leaves
salt and pepper
freshly chopped parsley for garnish

Serves 4

Slice the rollmop herrings and arrange them in a dish with the onion rings. Mix together the oil, vinegar, lemon juice and fish seasoning and pour over the herrings. Leave for 1 hour, basting with the dressing occasionally.

Cook the potatoes in boiling, salted water until just tender. Drain and cool them, then mix together the potatoes and beetroot. In a small bowl, combine the soured cream, ground bay, fennel and seasoning. If you are using dried fennel, reconstitute it in 10 ml (2 tsps) boiling water first. Fold the soured cream dressing through the potato and beetroot. Spoon the salad into a serving dish and sprinkle liberally with the chopped parsley. Serve with the rollmop herrings.

Supper salad with eggs

1 head celery, washed and sliced
4 carrots, pared and grated
a few radishes, washed and sliced
½ cucumber, sliced
4 eggs, hardboiled and sliced
paprika for garnish

For the dressing

300 ml (½ pt) natural yoghurt
5 ml (1 level tsp) paprika
5 ml (1 level tsp) sugar
15 ml (1 tbsp) lemon juice
15 ml (1 tbsp) orange juice
salt and pepper
5 ml (1 level tsp) dried parsley or 15 ml
  (1 tbsp) fresh chopped parsley

Serves 4

Combine all the ingredients for the dressing. Toss together the celery, carrots, radishes and cucumber. Add half the dressing to the celery mixture and gently fold it in. Put the salad in a serving dish, arrange hardboiled eggs on top and spoon the remaining dressing over the sliced eggs. Sprinkle with paprika and chill before serving.

Chicory and orange salad

4 heads chicory
2 oranges
30 ml (2 tbsps) clear honey
2·5 ml (½ level tsp) dried mint or 6 fresh
  mint leaves, chopped
1·25 ml (¼ level tsp) dried *fines herbes*
1·25 ml (¼ level tsp) onion salt
freshly ground black pepper
25 g (1 oz) shelled walnuts, coarsely
  chopped

Serves 4

Remove a few of the outer leaves from the chicory, wash and dry them and keep for garnishing. Slice the rest of the chicory finely and put it in a bowl. Remove the skin and the pith from the oranges and cut them into segments, reserving any juice. Put the segments in the bowl with the sliced chicory. In a small bowl or cup, mix together 30 ml (2 tbsps) orange juice, the honey, mint, *fines herbes*, onion salt and pepper. Leave to infuse for 15 minutes, then add the walnuts and the dressing to the chicory and orange. Toss them well together. Arrange the reserved chicory leaves in a serving dish and spoon the sliced chicory, orange and walnuts over the top. Serve as a side salad.

Dressed courgettes and leek salad

30 ml (2 tbsps) corn oil
15 ml (1 tbsp) distilled vinegar
1·25 ml (¼ level tsp) dried oregano
1·25 ml (¼ level tsp) dried mixed herbs
  or 5 ml (1 tsp) fresh mixed herbs
1·25 ml (¼ level tsp) onion salt
1·25 ml (¼ level tsp) dried chives or 5 ml
  (1 tsp) fresh chopped chives
salt and freshly ground black pepper
350 g (12 oz) courgettes, wiped and
  trimmed
275 g (10 oz) leeks, thinly sliced and
  washed

Serves 4

Put oil, vinegar, herbs, onion salt, chives, salt and pepper into a screw topped jar. Shake well then leave to infuse for ½ hour. Slice the courgettes 0·5 cm (¼ in) thick. Blanch them in boiling water until tender but still crisp – about 2 minutes. Drain and pat them dry. Blanch the leeks in boiling water for about 2 minutes. Drain well and add to the courgettes. Shake the dressing until it is creamy and pour it over the vegetables whilst they are still warm. Toss lightly, then chill before serving.

Salade niçoise

225 g (8 oz) tomatoes, skinned
½ a small cucumber, wiped and thinly sliced
salt and freshly ground black pepper
5 ml (1 level tsp) dried basil or 15 ml (1 tbsp) chopped fresh basil
5 ml (1 level tsp) dried parsley or 15 ml (1 tbsp) chopped fresh parsley
grated rind of 1 lemon
100 g (4 oz) French beans, cooked
50 g (2 oz) black olives, stoned and chopped
1·25 ml (¼ level tsp) minced garlic or ½ small clove garlic, skinned and crushed
60 ml (4 tbsps) French dressing
8 anchovy fillets, halved lengthwise
brown bread and butter
quarters of lemon

Serves 4

Slice the tomatoes and layer them with the cucumber on a shallow serving dish; season well and sprinkle with the herbs and lemon rind. Pile the French beans in the centre of the dish, scatter the olives over and season again. Add the garlic to the dressing and pour it over the salad. Arrange the anchovy fillets in a lattice pattern over the salad and allow to stand for about ½ hour before serving so that the flavours blend. Serve with brown bread and butter and lemon.

Italian pepper salad

2 green peppers
2 red peppers
30 ml (2 tbsps) red wine vinegar
30 ml (2 tbsps) olive oil
5 ml (1 tsp) Worcestershire sauce
5 ml (1 level tsp) tomato paste
2·5 ml (½ level tsp) paprika
salt
pinch sugar
4 black olives, stoned and quartered

Serves 4

Slice the peppers and remove the core and seeds. Put the slices in a pan of cold water, bring to the boil then drain and cool. Meanwhile, make the dressing. Put all the remaining ingredients (except the olives) into a bowl and whisk well together. Arrange the cold peppers in a serving dish. Pour the dressing over and leave for ½ hour. Scatter the olives over the top. Serve as a side salad.

Desserts

Apricot crunch pudding

5 1-cm ($\frac{1}{2}$-in) slices from a small loaf of
  bread
100 g (4 oz) butter or margarine
439-g (15$\frac{1}{2}$-oz) can apricot halves,
  drained (reserve 45 ml, 3 tbsps, juice)
5 ml (1 level tsp) ground cinnamon
5 ml (1 level tsp) ground nutmeg
90 ml (5 level tbsps) clear honey
25 g (1 oz) cornflakes
whipped cream or vanilla ice-cream for
  serving

Serves 4–5

Trim off the crusts and cut the bread
into 1-cm ($\frac{1}{2}$-in) cubes. Melt 50 g (2 oz)
butter in a pan and fry the bread a little
at a time, until golden; add more butter
as needed – up to 25 g (1 oz). When the
croûtons are ready, place them in a 1·1-l
(2-pt) ovenproof dish. Add apricots
and reserved juice to the bread cubes
and mix lightly together. Add the rest
of the butter to the pan with the spices
and honey. Fold the cornflakes into the
honey butter and spoon over the apricots. Bake in the oven at 180°C (350°F)
mark 4 for about 20 minutes. Serve
warm with whipped cream or vanilla
ice-cream.

Dutch apple pudding

225 g (8 oz) self raising flour
2·5 ml ($\frac{1}{2}$ level tsp) salt
100 g (4 oz) shredded suet
about 120 ml (8 tbsps) water
800 g (1$\frac{3}{4}$ lb) cooking apples
40 g (1$\frac{1}{2}$ oz) currants
40 g (1$\frac{1}{2}$ oz) sultanas
100 g (4 oz) granulated sugar
5 ml (1 level tsp) apple pie spice
22 ml (1$\frac{1}{2}$ level tbsps) cornflour

Serves 6

Half-fill a steamer or large pan with
water and put it on to boil. Grease a
1·4-l (2$\frac{1}{2}$-pt) pudding basin. Sift the
flour and salt together into a basin. Mix
in the suet and bind the mixture with
enough water to give a soft but not
sticky dough. Knead the pastry lightly
on a floured surface. Roll out two
thirds of the pastry and use it to line the
basin in the usual way.

Peel, core and thickly slice the apples.
Mix the remaining ingredients together
and toss the apples in the sugar mixture.
Pack them into the basin and top with
the remaining pastry. Seal the edges
well, cover with greased greaseproof
paper and kitchen foil and cook in the
saucepan for 2$\frac{1}{2}$ hours – keep the water on
the boil and the pan covered. Top up
the water level from time to time with
boiling water. To serve, remove the
foil and paper and turn out the pudding
on to a flat serving plate.

Apple and fig pie

225 g (8 oz) plain flour
pinch of salt
150 g (5 oz) butter or margarine
water to mix
700 g (1$\frac{1}{2}$ lb) cooking apples, peeled and
  cored
100 g (4 oz) dried figs, chopped
45 ml (3 level tbsps) sugar
15 ml (1 level tbsp) plain flour
2·5 ml ($\frac{1}{2}$ level tsp) ground cinnamon
1·25 ml ($\frac{1}{4}$ level tsp) ground nutmeg
pinch of ground cloves or 3–4 whole
  cloves
30–45 ml (2–3 tbsps) water
milk and caster sugar, for glazing

Serves 4–5

Sift the flour and salt into a bowl. Rub
the fat into the flour until the mixture

say Schwartz and be sure

resembles fine breadcrumbs and stir in just sufficient cold water to make a firm dough. Cover and leave it in a cool place to rest. Slice the apples into a basin, add the figs and sift over the sugar, flour and spices. Mix well together. Put the apples into a buttered 1·1-l (2-pt) pie dish. Sprinkle 30–45 ml (2–3 tbsps) water over the filling. Roll out the pastry and use it to cover the pie in the usual way. Decorate the top with pastry trimmings. Brush it with the milk and sprinkle with caster sugar. Bake in the oven at 220°C (425°F) mark 7 for 15 minutes, then reduce the heat to 180°C (350°F) mark 4 for a further 30 minutes. Serve warm.

Sesame seed and almond flan

For the pastry
50 g (2 oz) butter or margarine
50 g (2 oz) caster sugar
1 standard egg
175 g (6 oz) plain flour

For the filling
45–60 ml (3–4 level tbsps) apricot jam
100 g (4 oz) butter or margarine
100 g (4 oz) caster sugar
1 standard egg
75 g (3 oz) ground almonds
25 g (1 oz) plain flour
20 ml (4 level tsps) sesame seeds
1·25 ml ($\frac{1}{4}$ tsp) almond essence, optional

Serves 6–8

Cream the fat and sugar together, beat in the egg, stir in the flour and work together to form a stiff dough. Roll out the dough and use it to line a 23-cm (9-in) loose base fluted French flan tin. Reserve the trimmings. Spread the jam over the pastry base.

For the filling, cream together the fat and sugar until light and fluffy. Beat in the egg and stir in the ground almonds and flour. Add 10 ml (2 level tsps) of the sesame seeds and the almond essence if you wish. Spread the almond mixture over the jam. Sprinkle the remaining 10 ml (2 level tsps) of the sesame seeds over the almond mixture. Roll out the pastry trimmings and, using a small heart shaped or star cutter, stamp out enough shapes to form a circle round the outer edge of the flan. Bake it in the oven at 180°C (350°F) mark 4 for about 30 minutes.

Cherry strudel

For strudel dough
225 g (8 oz) plain flour
2·5 ml ($\frac{1}{2}$ level tsp) salt
150 ml ($\frac{1}{4}$ pt) lukewarm water
1 egg, beaten
1·25 ml ($\frac{1}{4}$ tsp) white vinegar
25 g (1 oz) butter, melted

For filling
2 425-g (15-oz) cans stoned morello cherries, drained, or 450 g (1 lb) fresh dark cherries, stoned and halved
10 ml (2 level tsps) grated lemon rind
454-g (1-lb) can sweetened apple purée
5 ml (1 level tsp) mixed spice
2·5 ml ($\frac{1}{2}$ level tsp) ground cinnamon
50 g (2 oz) butter, melted
50 g (2 oz) fresh white breadcrumbs
100 g (4 oz) ground almonds
icing sugar

Serves 8–10

Sift together the flour and salt into a bowl. Combine the water, egg, vinegar and butter and pour the liquid into the flour. Stir well until the mixture becomes a sticky dough. Turn it out on to a floured surface and knead for about 5 minutes or until the dough becomes smooth and elastic. Shape it into a ball and leave it on the floured surface covered with a warm basin, taking care it does not touch the dough. Leave it for 30 minutes.

Meanwhile make the filling. Mix together the cherries, lemon rind, apple purée and spices. Cover the table with a large clean cloth sprinkled with flour. Place the dough in the centre and brush it with melted butter. Roll it out until it is 3 mm ($\frac{1}{8}$ in) thick. Slip your hands under the dough and with your fingers kept together, gently pull from the centre with a stroking action to stretch the dough. When it is paper-thin, brush the surface with more melted butter and scatter over 25 g (1 oz) breadcrumbs. Sprinkle the ground almonds over a 12·5-cm (5-in) strip of strudel nearest to you. Spread the cherry filling over the almonds to within 5 cm (2 in) of the sides. Lift the cloth along the nearest edge and use it to roll the dough around the filling, like a Swiss roll. Tuck the unfilled ends under. Lift the roll on to a greased and floured baking sheet and form it into a horseshoe. Brush it with the remaining butter and sprinkle with breadcrumbs. Bake it in the oven at 200°C (400°F) mark 6 for 15 minutes, then reduce the heat to 180°C (350°F) mark 4 and cook for a further 30 minutes or until the strudel is crisp and brown. Dredge with icing sugar and serve warm.

Caribbean bananas

50 g (2 oz) butter
4 firm bananas, peeled
30 ml (2 level tbsps) demerara sugar
2·5 ml ($\frac{1}{2}$ level tsp) ground ginger
2·5 ml ($\frac{1}{2}$ level tsp) ground cinnamon
30 ml (2 tbsps) dark rum
pouring cream for serving

Serves 4

Melt the butter in a frying pan, add the whole bananas and fry them quickly for about 1 minute, turning once. Mix the remaining ingredients together and spread over the bananas. Continue to cook over a moderate heat until the bananas are soft and the sugar caramelises. Serve hot, with pouring cream.

Peach drop-cakes

225 g (8 oz) plain flour
10 ml (2 level tsps) baking powder
10 ml (2 level tsps) sugar
2·5 ml ($\frac{1}{2}$ level tsp) apple pie spice
good pinch salt
3 eggs, lightly beaten
150 ml ($\frac{1}{4}$ pt) milk
300 ml ($\frac{1}{2}$ pt) buttermilk
50 g (2 oz) butter, melted
425-g (15-oz) can peaches
50 g (2 oz) lard, for frying
honey or maple syrup, optional

Makes about 12

Sift the flour, baking powder, sugar, spice and salt together into a large bowl. Make a well in the centre of the flour and pour in the eggs, milk and buttermilk. Mix them together only long enough to blend, then stir in the melted butter. Do not overmix, the pancakes will be lighter if the batter is not too smooth. Drain the peaches, reserving the syrup. Chop the peaches and add them to the batter.

Heat a griddle or frying pan over a moderate heat. Grease it lightly with lard and pour the batter from a jug or a ladle on to the heated pan to form pancakes about 10 cm (4 in) across. Cook each one for 2–3 minutes until small bubbles have formed on the surface. Turn it with a spatula and cook for a further 1–2 minutes until golden brown. Stack them on a heated dish and serve with warmed peach syrup, honey or maple syrup.

Pears and orange pancakes

8 or 10 18-cm (7-in) pancakes, see note below
pared rind and juice of 1 large orange
10 whole cloves
300 ml ($\frac{1}{2}$ pt) water
30 ml (2 level tbsps) caster sugar
3-4 firm dessert pears, peeled, cored and chopped
10 ml (2 tsps) lemon juice
25 ml ($1\frac{1}{2}$ level tbsps) cornflour

Serves 4–5

Make the pancakes and keep them hot. Place the thinly pared orange rind, cloves and water in a saucepan. Heat gently until almost boiling, then remove the pan from the heat, cover it and leave to infuse for 30 minutes. Discard the cloves and orange rind. Add the sugar and chopped pears to the flavoured water and simmer gently until the pears are tender. Drain the pears and add the orange and lemon juice to the syrup. Make the syrup up to 300 ml ($\frac{1}{2}$ pt) with water, if necessary. Blend the cornflour with a little of the syrup until smooth, heat the rest of the syrup until almost boiling then stir it into the cornflour mixture. Return it to the pan and heat gently, stirring, until the sauce thickens. Boil for 1 minute, stirring, then add the chopped pears.

Divide the mixture between the pancakes and either roll them up or fold them into fours. Place the filled pancakes in an ovenproof dish and spoon any remaining sauce over. Bake in the oven at 200°C (400°F) mark 6 for 10–15 minutes, to heat through. Serve hot, with pouring cream if you wish.

Note The pancakes are made with 300 ml ($\frac{1}{2}$ pt) milk or milk and water, 125 g (4 oz) plain flour, a pinch of salt and one egg.

Christmas pudding

175 g (6 oz) plain flour
2·5 ml ($\frac{1}{2}$ level tsp) ground ginger
2·5 ml ($\frac{1}{2}$ level tsp) ground cinnamon
2·5 ml ($\frac{1}{2}$ level tsp) grated whole nutmeg
100 g (4 oz) apple, peeled and cored
75 g (3 oz) fresh white breadcrumbs
100 g (4 oz) shredded suet
100 g (4 oz) stoned raisins, chopped
225 g (8 oz) currants, cleaned
225 g (8 oz) sultanas, cleaned
75 g (3 oz) demerara sugar
grated rind of 1 lemon
grated rind of 1 orange
2 eggs, beaten
200 ml ($\frac{1}{3}$ pt) brown ale

Serves 6–8

Grease a 1·1-l (2-pt) pudding basin. Sift together the flour, ginger, cinnamon and nutmeg. Dice the apple and add it to the flour, along with the breadcrumbs, suet, dried fruit, sugar, lemon and orange rinds. Mix the ingredients well. Gradually stir in the beaten eggs and ale and stir thoroughly. If possible leave the mixture to stand overnight.

Turn the mixture into the prepared basin, then cover with greased greaseproof paper and kitchen foil or a pudding cloth. Tie the foil or cloth firmly in place with string. Either place the bowl in a pan with water halfway up the sides and, after bringing to the boil, reduce heat and boil gently for about 6 hours, or place in a steamer and cook for

8 hours. A piece of lemon in the water will prevent discoloration of the pan. Top up with more boiling water at intervals. To store, leave the grease-proof paper in position, but re-wrap with fresh foil or pudding cloth. On the day you wish to eat it, re-boil for about 3 hours.

Old fashioned custard tart

200 g (7 oz) plain flour
pinch salt
100 g (3½ oz) butter or margarine
1·25 ml (¼ level tsp) ground cinnamon
15 ml (1 level tbsp) icing sugar, sifted
water to mix
400 ml (¾ pt) milk
3 standard eggs
25–50 g (1–2 oz) caster sugar
whole nutmeg

Serves 4–6

Sift the flour and salt into a bowl. Rub in the fat until the mixture resembles fine breadcrumbs. Stir in the cinnamon and icing sugar and add enough water to mix to a stiff but manageable consistency. Roll out the dough and use it to line a 20·5-cm (8-in) fluted flan ring placed on a baking sheet. Bake 'blind' in the oven at 220°C (425°F) mark 7 for 10 minutes. Remove the baking beans and greaseproof paper. Warm the milk in a saucepan but do not boil it. Whisk the eggs and sugar lightly in a bowl and pour on the hot milk, stirring all the time. Strain the mixture into the flan case. Grate a little nutmeg on top and bake in the oven at 170°C (325°F) mark 3 for about 45 minutes, or until the custard is set and firm to the touch. Serve warm or cold.

Plum crumble

538-g (1-lb 3-oz) can plums
10 ml (2 level tsps) cornflour
2·5–5 ml (½–1 level tsp) mixed spice
75 g (3 oz) plain flour
75 g (3 oz) rolled oats
pinch of salt
75 g (3 oz) butter or margarine
25 g (1 oz) sugar
25 g (1 oz) chopped almonds

Serves 4

Drain the plums, reserving the juice. In a small bowl blend together the cornflour, mixed spice and 15 ml (1 tbsp) plum juice. Bring the remaining juice to the boil and pour it on to the blended corn-flour. Return it to the heat and bring to the boil, stirring. Put the plums into a 1·1-l (2-pt) ovenproof pie dish. Pour the juice over the plums.

Put flour, oats and salt into a bowl. Rub in the butter. Add the sugar and almonds and mix well together. Sprinkle this crumble over plums and bake in the oven at 200°C (400°F) mark 6 for 20–25 minutes.

Spotted Dick

75 g (3 oz) self raising flour
a pinch of salt
2·5 ml (½ level tsp) ground ginger
1·25 ml (¼ level tsp) ground cloves
75 g (3 oz) fresh white breadcrumbs
75 g (3 oz) shredded suet
50 g (2 oz) caster sugar
175 g (6 oz) currants, cleaned
60–90 ml (4–6 tbsps) milk

Serves 4

Put a steamer or large saucepan with water on to boil. Sift together the flour, salt and spices into a bowl and add the breadcrumbs, suet, sugar and currants. Make a well in the centre and add enough milk to give a fairly soft dough. Form the dough into a roll on a well-floured board, wrap it loosely in greased grease-proof paper then in foil, sealing the ends firmly. Steam rapidly for $1\frac{1}{2}$–2 hours. Unwrap the pudding, put it in a hot dish and serve with custard or a white sauce flavoured with cinnamon or grated lemon rind.

Alternatively, make the mixture to a soft dropping consistency and steam it for $1\frac{1}{2}$–2 hours in a greased 900-ml ($1\frac{1}{2}$-pt) basin, covered with greased foil or greaseproof paper.

Steamed date and walnut pudding

175 g (6 oz) self raising flour
2·5 ml ($\frac{1}{2}$ level tsp) ground cinnamon
1·25 ml ($\frac{1}{4}$ level tsp) ground nutmeg
75 g (3 oz) butter or margarine
75 g (3 oz) soft brown sugar
50 g (2 oz) stoned dates, chopped
50 g (2 oz) shelled walnuts, chopped
1 large egg, beaten
60 ml (4 tbsps) milk
golden syrup or custard for serving

Serves 4–5

Sift the flour, cinnamon and the nutmeg into a bowl. Rub in the fat until the mixture resembles fine breadcrumbs. Stir in the sugar, dates, and walnuts. Add the egg and milk and mix to a soft consistency. Turn the mixture into a lightly buttered 500-ml (1-pt) pudding basin. Cover with greased foil or grease-proof paper and a pudding cloth. Half-fill a large saucepan with boiling water, put the pudding basin in and, over a low heat, steam it for $1\frac{1}{2}$–2 hours. Remove the coverings, turn the pudding out on

to a warm dish and serve with golden syrup or custard.

Pumpkin chiffon pie

For the pastry
200 g (7 oz) plain flour
pinch salt
50 g (2 oz) butter or margarine
50 g (2 oz) lard
water to mix

For the filling
700 g ($1\frac{1}{2}$ lb) pumpkin, bought weight
100 g (4 oz) soft brown sugar
just under 150 ml ($\frac{1}{4}$ pt) water
5 ml (1 level tsp) ground cinnamon
2·5 ml ($\frac{1}{2}$ level tsp) ground nutmeg
pinch ground cloves
1·25 ml ($\frac{1}{4}$ level tsp) ground ginger
300 ml ($\frac{1}{2}$ pt) double cream
25 ml ($1\frac{1}{2}$ level tbsps) powdered gelatine
45–60 ml (3–4 tbsps) water
2 egg whites

For decoration
pecan halves or whole hazelnuts
whipped cream

Serves 6–8

To make the pastry, sift together the flour and salt into a bowl. Rub in the fats until the mixture resembles fine breadcrumbs. Add enough water to mix to a firm but manageable dough. Roll it out and use it to line a 23-cm (9-in) straight sided flan dish or flan ring. Bake 'blind' in the oven at 220°C (425°F) mark 7 for 20 minutes. Remove the baking beans and return the flan case to the oven for a further few minutes until the pastry is dried out and crisp. Allow the pastry case to cool.

To make the filling, remove the rind from the pumpkin. Cut the flesh into cubes and place in a saucepan with the sugar, water and spices. Simmer it gently for about 15 minutes until soft. Purée the mixture in an electric blender or pass it through a sieve. Whip the cream until thick but not stiff and fold the cream into the cooled pumpkin purée. Sprinkle the gelatine over the water in a small bowl and place it in a pan in a little hot water. When the gelatine has dissolved, stir it into the pumpkin cream. Whisk the egg whites until stiff, fold them gently into the pumpkin cream using a metal spoon and pour the mixture into the pastry case. Refrigerate until just set; do not leave for longer. Bring the pie to room temperature to serve. Decorate it with whipped cream and pecan halves or whole hazel nuts.

Rhubarb and ginger fool

450 g (1 lb) rhubarb, trimmed
15 ml (1 level tbsp) granulated sugar
$\frac{1}{2}$ 127-g (1-pt) jelly tablet
15 ml (1 level tbsp) custard powder
30 ml (2 level tbsps) granulated sugar
150 ml ($\frac{1}{4}$ pt) milk
2·5 ml ($\frac{1}{2}$ level tsp) ground ginger
30 ml (2 tbsps) ginger syrup
2 pieces stem ginger, finely chopped
150 ml ($\frac{1}{4}$ pt) double cream
1 egg white

Serves 6

Cut the rhubarb into short lengths. Place it in a saucepan with the granulated sugar and cook gently until the fruit softens. Scissor-snip the jelly tablet into the saucepan and continue heating until the jelly melts; do not boil. Remove from the heat. Blend the custard powder and caster sugar with a little of the milk.

Heat the remaining milk in a saucepan. Pour over the blended custard, stir and return to the heat to thicken. Combine the rhubarb, custard, ground ginger and syrup and purée in an electric blender or pass through a sieve. In a bowl, combine the purée with two-thirds of the chopped ginger. Cool. Whip the cream until thick but not stiff. Stiffly whisk the egg white. Fold the cream into the egg white and then fold this into the rhubarb mixture. Divide between six sundae dishes and top with the remaining ginger. Chill before serving.

Cinnamon and soured cream raisin pie

200 g (7 oz) digestive biscuits
100 g ($3\frac{1}{2}$ oz) unsalted butter, melted
2 eggs, separated
100 g (4 oz) cottage cheese, sieved
150 ml (5 fl oz) soured cream
2·5 ml ($\frac{1}{2}$ tsp) vanilla essence
30 ml (2 level tbsps) caster sugar
5 ml (1 level tsp) ground cinnamon
2·5 ml ($\frac{1}{2}$ level tsp) ground nutmeg
100 g (4 oz) seedless raisins
icing sugar

Serves 6

Crush the biscuits to a fine crumb, using a rolling pin. Combine the crumbs with melted butter. Press the mixture against the sides and base of a 23-cm (9-in) round ovenproof glass flan dish and chill it while you make the filling.

Put the egg yolks, cheese, soured cream, vanilla essence, sugar, spices and raisins into a bowl and stir well together. Whisk the egg whites until stiff and fold them gently into the filling using a metal spoon. Pour it into the biscuit crumb case. Bake in the oven at

180°C (350°F) mark 4 for 35–40 minutes until set and lightly browned. Leave the pie until cold. Dust with sifted icing sugar before serving. Eat this pie the same day you make it.

Old English ice cream

300 ml ($\frac{1}{2}$ pt) milk
60 ml (4 level tbsps) honey
2 eggs, beaten
100 g (4 oz) seedless raisins
7·5 ml (1$\frac{1}{2}$ level tsps) ground nutmeg
60 ml (4 level tbsps) flaked toasted almonds
300 ml ($\frac{1}{2}$ pt) double cream

Serves 6

Heat the milk and honey together and pour them on to the eggs, stirring. Return the mixture to the saucepan and heat gently without boiling, stirring until the mixture thickens. Strain this custard into a bowl and add the raisins, nutmeg and flaked almonds. Allow it to cool, then half-whip the double cream and fold into the mixture; pour into a freezing tray and freeze. Before serving leave the ice cream for about 1 hour in the refrigerator to allow time for it to 'come to'.

*Fresh fruit salad with honey

1 small melon
275 g (10 oz) fresh pineapple
312-g (11-oz) can mandarin oranges
60 ml (4 level tbsps) honey
1·25 2·5 ml ($\frac{1}{4}$ $\frac{1}{2}$ level tsp) cardamom seeds, crushed

Serves 4–6

Halve the melon, discard the seeds and scoop out the flesh into balls using a melon baller, or dice it. Place the fruit in a bowl with any juice. Discard the leaf top from the pineapple and cut the fruit into 1-cm ($\frac{1}{2}$-in) slices. With a small sharp knife, remove the skin from the slices and the centre core (an apple corer or small cutter is useful for this job). Cut the fruit into small pieces and add it to the melon. Drain the mandarin juice into a pan and add the mandarins to the other fruit. Heat the mandarin juice with the honey and crushed cardamom seeds. Bring it to the boil, remove from the heat and allow to cool. Strain the syrup over the fruit and chill before serving.

Bramble syllabub

350 g (12 oz) blackberries, fresh or frozen, thawed
15 ml (1 level tbsp) sugar
2·5 ml ($\frac{1}{2}$ level tsp) ground mace
2 egg whites
100 g (4 oz) caster sugar
juice of $\frac{1}{2}$ lemon
150 ml ($\frac{1}{4}$ pt) dry white wine
300 ml ($\frac{1}{2}$ pt) double cream, whipped
whole blackberries to decorate

Serves 6

Pick over and wash the fresh blackberries; dry them well. Put the blackberries in a heavy pan with the 15 ml (1 level tbsp) sugar and the ground mace. Heat gently until the fruit is soft but still whole. Allow it to cool, then spoon the fruit into the bases of six stemmed glasses. (If there is too much juice, reduce this by boiling rapidly, then spoon it over the fruit.) Whisk the egg whites stiffly and fold in the caster sugar, lemon juice, wine and whipped cream. Spoon the mixture carefully over the fruit in the glasses. Chill for up to 1 hour and serve decorated with whole blackberries.

Note This dessert is best if made only 1–2 hours before serving, as the topping separates and becomes more liquid on standing.

Dried fruit compote

450-g (1-lb) selection of dried fruits (e.g. prunes, figs, apples, apricots, pears)
60 ml (4 tbsps) clear honey
6 whole cloves
2 cinnamon sticks
2·5 ml ($\frac{1}{2}$ level tsp) mixed spice
single cream for serving

Serves 6–8

Put the dried fruit into a bowl. Cover with water and soak overnight. The next day drain the fruit, reserving 300 ml ($\frac{1}{2}$ pt) water. Place the fruit, water, honey, cloves, cinnamon sticks and the mixed spice in a saucepan. If you prefer the cinnamon sticks and cloves may be tied in a muslin bag for easy removal. Bring the water to the boil, cover, reduce the heat and simmer for about 10 minutes. Serve warm or chilled, with single cream.

Spiced pears

300 ml ($\frac{1}{2}$ pt) red wine
60–90 ml (4–6 tbsps) red wine vinegar
225 g (8 oz) caster sugar
2 cinnamon sticks (about 7·5 cm, 3 in) or 5 ml (1 level tsp) ground cinnamon
6 whole cloves
4 medium sized firm ripe dessert pears
single cream for serving

Serves 4

Put the wine, vinegar, sugar, cinnamon and cloves in a saucepan. Bring them to the boil over a moderate heat, stirring until the sugar dissolves. Boil this syrup for 5 minutes, then reduce the heat to low. Peel the pears, cut them in half lengthways and remove the cores. Add the pear halves to the syrup and turn them over with a spoon until they are evenly coated. Cover the pan and simmer gently for about 10 minutes or until the pears are just tender. Remove the pan from the heat and let it cool. Put the pears and syrup in a serving dish. Chill. Serve with single cream.

Minted grapefruit sorbet

100 g (4 oz) sugar
300 ml ($\frac{1}{2}$ pt) water
2·5 ml ($\frac{1}{2}$ level tsp) dried mint or 7·5 ml (1$\frac{1}{2}$ tsps) chopped fresh mint
538-g (1-lb 3-oz) can sweetened grapefruit segments
90 ml (6 tbsps) sweet white Vermouth
2 egg whites

Serves 6

Dissolve the sugar in the water in a saucepan over a low heat. Bring to the boil and boil gently for 10 minutes. Add the mint, cover and leave to cool. Purée the grapefruit with its juice in a blender to make about 500 ml (1 pt) purée. Stir in the Vermouth and add the strained syrup. Pour the grapefruit mixture into a container suitable for freezing, such as an ice cube tray without the divisions, and freeze until mushy. Turn it into a bowl and beat with a fork. Whisk the egg whites until stiff and fold them into the grapefruit mush. Return it to the container and freeze. Use straight from the freezer.

Creamed rice amontillado

500 ml (1 pt) milk
75 g (3 oz) short grain rice
40–50 g (1½–2 oz) sugar
1·25 ml (¼ level tsp) ground allspice
30 ml (2 tbsps) sherry
300 ml (½ pt) double cream
50 g (2 oz) flaked almonds, toasted

Serves 4–5

Put the milk, rice and sugar into a saucepan. Bring them slowly to the boil, stirring, and simmer gently for about 20 minutes or until the rice is cooked. Leave the pan uncovered and stir occasionally. Remove it from the heat, stir in the allspice and sherry and leave to cool. Whip the cream until thick but not stiff. Fold the cream into the rice mixture and turn it into individual serving dishes. Top with the almonds and chill before serving.

Cakes and Biscuits

Ginger snaps

100 g (4 oz) butter
60 ml (4 level tbsps) golden syrup
225 g (8 oz) self raising flour
20 ml (4 level tsps) ground ginger
5 ml (1 level tsp) ground cinnamon
1·25 ml ($\frac{1}{4}$ level tsp) ground cloves
5 ml (1 level tsp) bicarbonate of soda
30 ml (2 level tbsps) caster sugar
about 30 blanched almond halves

Makes about 30

Melt the butter and golden syrup to-gether in a small pan. Sift together into a bowl the flour, ginger, cinnamon, cloves and bicarbonate of soda. Add the sugar and stir in the slightly cooled butter and syrup, mixing well. Form the mixture into about 30 small balls between the palms of your hands and place them on greased baking sheets, leaving enough space between each one to allow for spreading. Place a halved almond on top of each ball and press down lightly. Bake in the oven at 190°C (375°F) mark 5 for 12–15 minutes. Cool them on a wire rack.

Fluted gingerbread loaf

225 g (8 oz) plain flour
2·5 ml ($\frac{1}{2}$ level tsp) salt
25 ml (5 level tsps) ground ginger
2·5 ml ($\frac{1}{2}$ level tsp) baking powder
2·5 ml ($\frac{1}{2}$ level tsp) bicarbonate of soda
100 g (4 oz) light, soft brown sugar
75 g (3 oz) butter
15 ml (1 tbsp) treacle
150 g (5 oz) golden syrup
150 ml ($\frac{1}{4}$ pt) milk
1 egg, beaten
4–5 pieces preserved stem ginger

Grease thoroughly a 28-cm by 10-cm (11-in by 4-in) ridged oblong tin, 1·1-l (2-pt) capacity. Sift together the flour, salt, ground ginger, baking powder and bicarbonate of soda into a bowl. Make a well in the centre. Put the sugar, butter, treacle and golden syrup in a saucepan and heat gently until of an even consistency. Do not boil. Remove the pan from the heat and add the milk and egg. Pour this mixture into the dry ingredients and beat well until smooth. Turn it into the prepared tin and bake in the oven at 170°C (325°F) mark 3 for about 1 hour 10 minutes. Allow the loaf to cool slightly, then turn it out to cool on a wire rack. Decorate with groups of sliced stem ginger.
Note If the special tin is not available, use a 26·5-cm by 11·5-cm (10$\frac{1}{2}$-in by 4$\frac{1}{2}$-in) top measurement, sloping sided plain loaf tin.

Raisin streusel cake

For topping

100 g (4 oz) butter
100 g (4 oz) caster sugar
100 g (4 oz) plain flour
5 ml (1 level tsp) ground cinnamon

For cake

225 g (8 oz) self raising flour
2·5 ml ($\frac{1}{2}$ level tsp) ground nutmeg
pinch ground cloves
1·25 ml ($\frac{1}{4}$ level tsp) salt
100 g (4 oz) butter
100 g (4 oz) caster sugar
3 eggs
60 ml (4 tbsps) milk
225 g (8 oz) seedless raisins

Line the base of a 24-cm (9$\frac{1}{2}$-in) round, loose-bottomed cake tin and grease and flour it. To make the topping, put the butter, sugar, flour and cinnamon into a bowl. Rub together until the mixture resembles coarse breadcrumbs. Set aside.

To make the cake, sift together the flour, nutmeg, cloves and salt. Cream the butter and sugar together until light and fluffy. Beat in the eggs one at a time, then fold in the flour. Stir in the milk and raisins and mix well together. Put the mixture into the prepared tin and smooth the top. Sprinkle the crumb topping evenly over the mixture. Bake in the oven at 190°C (375°F) mark 5 for 40–50 minutes. Remove the cake from the tin to cool.

Poppy seed yeast cake

25 ml (1½ tbsps) lukewarm water
25 g (1 oz) fresh yeast or 30 ml (2 level tbsps) dried yeast
45 ml (3 tbsps) milk
50 g (2 oz) granulated sugar
275 g (10 oz) plain flour
1 egg
50 g (2 oz) butter, softened and cut in small pieces

For filling
100 g (4 oz) poppy seeds
25 g (1 oz) chopped almonds
50 g (2 oz) seedless raisins, chopped
finely grated rind of 1 lemon
finely grated rind of 1 medium orange
75 ml (5 tbsps) milk
100 g (4 oz) granulated sugar
15 ml (1 level tbsp) plain flour
1 egg, separated
15 ml (1 tbsp) single cream or top of the milk
15 ml (1 tbsp) melted butter

For topping
milk
icing sugar

Pour the lukewarm water into a small bowl and crumble in the fresh yeast or sprinkle the dried. Leave to stand for 5 minutes, then stir to dissolve it completely, leave in a warm place for another 3–5 minutes until mixture begins to froth. In a saucepan warm the milk to dissolve the sugar then allow it to cool. Put the yeast mixture in a large bowl, stir in the milk and sugar and beat in 250 g (9 oz) of the flour alternately with the egg and butter. Mix until the dough can be gathered into a compact ball, then transfer it to a work surface sprinkled with the remaining flour and knead the dough until smooth. Shape it into a ball and place in a mixing bowl. Add enough cold water to cover the dough by about 4 cm (1½ in) and leave it until the top of the ball of dough has risen above the surface of the water. This takes 15–45 minutes depending on the room temperature. Remove the dough from the water and pat the surface dry with kitchen paper. Knead it again for 5–10 minutes, until it is smooth and elastic. Place it in a lightly greased bowl, cover loosely with a tea towel and leave to rise in a warm place for about 30 minutes, until double in size.

To make the filling, grind the poppy seeds in an electric blender or use a pestle and mortar. Mix the poppy seeds with the almonds, raisins, lemon and orange rind. Whisk together the milk, sugar and flour. Put these into a saucepan and bring to the boil, stirring continuously. Remove from the heat and pour the hot mixture over the poppy seed mixture. Add the egg yolk and cream or top of the milk and mix thoroughly. Whisk the egg white until stiff and fold it into the mixture.

When the dough has risen, punch it down briefly to break up the air bubbles. Place it on a lightly floured surface and roll out to a rectangle about 20·5 cm by 30·5 cm (8 in by 12 in). Spread the filling evenly over the dough to within 1 cm ($\frac{1}{2}$ in) of the edges and dribble the melted butter over. First roll one 20·5 cm (8 in) side to the centre, like a Swiss roll, then roll the opposite side to the centre in the same way. Firmly holding both sides together, turn the cake over so that the seam is on the bottom when the cake is set in the tin. Put it in a loaf tin measuring 24 cm by 13 cm by 7·5 cm (9$\frac{1}{2}$ in by 5$\frac{1}{2}$ in by 3 in). Brush the top with milk.

Bake it in the oven at 190°C (375°F) mark 5 for about 1 hour until golden brown and crusty. Let it cool in the tin, then turn it out and dust with icing sugar. Let it cool completely before slicing. Serve whilst really fresh.

Almond tutti frutti cake

175 g (6 oz) butter or margarine (or half and half)
175 g (6 oz) caster sugar
3 eggs, beaten
5 ml (1 tsp) almond essence
175 g (6 oz) self raising flour
2·5-cm (1-in) piece of angelica
6 glacé cherries
30 ml (2 level tbsps) flaked almonds

For filling
40 g (1$\frac{1}{2}$ oz) butter
75 g (3 oz) icing sugar
2·5 ml ($\frac{1}{2}$ tsp) almond essence

Grease and base-line two 20·5-cm (8-in) straight sided sandwich tins. Cream the fat. Add the sugar and beat until light and fluffy. Beat in the eggs gradually, with the almond essence. Lightly beat in the flour. Divide the mixture evenly between the tins and level the surfaces. Scissor snip the angelica and the cherries

into small pieces and scatter with the almonds over the surface of one cake only. Bake at 180°C (350°F) mark 4 for about 25 minutes or until spongy to the touch. Turn out the cakes and cool them on a wire rack.

For the filling, cream the butter and gradually beat in the sifted icing sugar and almond essence. Use filling to sandwich the cakes together, placing the sponge with the cherries and angelica on the top.

Caraway cobbler ring cake

For topping
50 g (2 oz) butter or margarine
50 g (2 oz) blended white vegetable
75 g (3 oz) light soft brown sugar
1 egg, beaten
200 g (7 oz) self raising flour
grated rind $\frac{1}{2}$ lemon
25 g (1 oz) cornflakes, crushed
7·5 ml (1$\frac{1}{2}$ level tsps) caraway seeds

For base
100 g (4 oz) butter or margarine
100 g (4 oz) caster sugar
2 large eggs, beaten
grated rind $\frac{1}{2}$ lemon
100 g (4 oz) self raising flour

Grease and base line a 19-cm, 1·4-l (7$\frac{1}{2}$-in, 2$\frac{1}{2}$-pt) angel ring mould with sloping sides. For the topping, cream the fats and sugar together until light and fluffy. Beat in the egg. Gradually add the sifted flour with the lemon rind and half the cornflakes. Combine the remaining cornflakes with the caraway seeds.

Lightly flour your hands. Shape the dough into small balls and toss them in cornflake mixture until covered, then put them in the refrigerator to chill.

For the base, cream the fat and sugar

until light and fluffy. Gradually add the eggs, beating well after each addition and stir in the lemon rind. Sift the flour over the creamed mixture and stir in gradually, then beat lightly. Spread the mixture in base of the tin and level the surface. Bake the sponge in the oven at 180°C (350°F) mark 4 for about 20 minutes. Remove it from the oven and quickly place the topping balls over the base. Return it to the oven and cook for a further 20 minutes or until firm and golden. Allow the cake to cool in the tin before easing round the edge with a knife and turning it out on to a wire rack to cool. Serve bobble top uppermost.

Cream filled cinnamon roll

3 eggs
100 g (4 oz) caster sugar
100 g (4 oz) plain flour
5 ml (1 level tsp) ground cinnamon
15 ml (1 tbsp) hot water
150 ml ($\frac{1}{4}$ pt) double cream
25 g (1 oz) preserved stem ginger, finely chopped
icing sugar

Grease and line a 33·5-cm by 23·5-cm (13$\frac{1}{4}$-in by 9$\frac{1}{4}$-in) Swiss roll tin. Whisk the eggs and sugar in a bowl over hot, not boiling, water until thick and creamy. Remove it from the heat and sift the flour and cinnamon directly over the egg mixture. Add the hot water and carefully and thoroughly fold in the flour, using a metal spoon. Pour the mixture into the prepared tin. Bake in the oven at 220°C (425°F) mark 7 for 7–9 minutes, until golden brown and firm.

Meanwhile have ready a sheet of greaseproof or non-stick paper. Place the paper on top of a damp tea towel and sprinkle it with caster sugar. Turn the sponge out on to the paper. Trim off the crusty edges with a sharp knife and roll up the sponge with the aid of the greaseproof paper, leaving the paper inside, and leave it to become cold. Whisk the cream until it just holds its shape and fold in the finely chopped ginger. Gently unroll the sponge and spread cream over almost to the edges. Roll it up again without the paper and liberally dust with sifted icing sugar. Mark the top with criss crosses with a very hot skewer. Eat the same day, served with a small fork.

Marmalade mace tea-bread

225 g (8 oz) self raising flour
pinch of salt
5 ml (1 level tsp) ground mace
100 g (4 oz) butter
100 g (4 oz) demerara sugar
1 egg, beaten
90 ml (6 tbsps) chunky marmalade
60 ml (4 tbsps) milk
3 crystallised orange slices

Grease and line a 24-cm by 14-cm (9$\frac{1}{2}$-in by 5$\frac{1}{2}$-in) top measurement loaf tin. Sift together the flour, salt and spice into a bowl. Rub in the fat until the mixture resembles fine crumbs. Add the demerara sugar. Stir in the egg and 60 ml (4 tbsps) marmalade and the milk. Turn the mixture into the prepared tin, level the surface and top with the halved slices of orange. Bake in the oven at 180°C (350°F) mark 4 for about 1 hour. Turn the loaf out on to a wire rack. While it is still warm, brush the surface with the remaining marmalade. Cool. Foil-wrap and store for up to one week.

Sultana and cherry spice cake

225 g (8 oz) butter or margarine
225 g (8 oz) dark soft brown sugar
4 eggs
225 g (8 oz) self raising flour
pinch of salt
5 ml (1 level tsp) ground allspice
5 ml (1 level tsp) ground ginger
100 g (4 oz) sultanas
50 g (2 oz) glacé cherries, chopped
50 g (2 oz) shelled walnuts, chopped

Grease and line a 23-cm by 18-cm (9-in by 7-in) deep cake tin. Cream together the butter and sugar until light and fluffy. Beat in the eggs, one at a time. Sift together the dry ingredients, add the fruit and nuts and fold these into the creamed mixture. Turn the mixture into the prepared tin and smooth the surface with the back of a spoon. Bake in the oven at 170°C (325°F) mark 3 for about 1½ hours. Cool for a while in the tin, then turn out the cake to finish cooling on a wire rack. Wrap in foil and store for up to 1 week.

Apple shortcakes

1 lemon
450 g (1 lb) cooking or crisp eating apples
225 g (8 oz) self raising flour
5 ml (1 level tsp) baking powder
75 g (3 oz) butter or margarine
60 ml (4 level tbsps) caster sugar
cold milk
5 ml (1 level tsp) apple pie spice
thin honey

Makes 8

Finely grate the rind from the lemon and squeeze the juice. Peel and thinly slice the apples and toss the slices in lemon juice. Sift together the flour and baking powder and rub in the fat. Add the grated lemon rind and 30 ml (2 tbsps) caster sugar. Blend it to a soft dough with a little cold milk, then roll out the dough and use it to line 8 shallow individual Yorkshire pudding type patty tins, four to a tray and about 10-cm (4-in) diameter, top measurement. Arrange apple slices over the scone bases. Blend together 30 ml (2 tbsps) caster sugar and the apple pie spice, and sprinkle it over the apples. Bake at 200°C (400°F) mark 6 for about 25 minutes. Whilst still warm, brush with thin honey.

Aniseed biscuits

2 eggs
225 g (8 oz) caster sugar
30 ml (2 level tbsps) aniseed
275 g (10 oz) plain flour
5 ml (1 level tsp) baking powder

Beat the eggs and sugar until thick and creamy. Gradually add the aniseed and the flour sifted with the baking powder and stir until the mixture is evenly blended. Turn out the dough on to a floured surface and knead quickly. The dough must not be moist, but rather dry. Roll out the dough 0.5–1 cm ($\frac{1}{4}$–$\frac{3}{8}$ in) thick and cut out biscuits with fancy cutters. Place the shapes on greased baking sheets and leave to rest uncovered for 24 hours in a dry, airy place. When ready for cooking, the biscuits should be dry and white on top, but damp underneath. Bake in the oven at 180°C (350°F) mark 4 for about 15 minutes. The biscuits should rise slightly but remain white.

These biscuits are a traditional German recipe, usually made at Christmas. They used to be made in ornate moulds of Christmas symbols such as St. Nicolas,

Angels and Christmas trees. Nowadays they are usually cut into star or bell shapes. The biscuits are much paler and of a firmer, drier texture than English biscuits.

Minted fruit fingers

200 g (7 oz) plain flour
pinch of salt
100 g (3½ oz) butter or margarine
30 ml (2 level tbsps) caster sugar
1 standard egg, beaten

For filling
40 g (1½ oz) butter or margarine
30 ml (2 level tbsps) caster sugar
100 g (4 oz) currants
5 ml (1 level tsp) dried mint

For glaze
milk
caster sugar

Makes 14–16

Sift the flour and salt into a basin. Rub in the butter until the mixture resembles fine breadcrumbs, then stir in the sugar. Add the egg and mix to a stiff dough. Roll the pastry out to two rectangles each measuring approximately 25·5 cm by 15 cm (10 in by 6 in).

To make the filling melt the butter and remove from the heat. Stir in the sugar, currants and mint. Place one of the pastry rectangles on a baking sheet. Spread the filling over the pastry to within 1 cm (½ in) of the edge. Brush the edges with water and place the other rectangle on top. Seal the edges well and pinch with the fingers or mark decoratively with a fork. Brush with milk and dredge with sugar. Bake in the oven at 200°C (400°F) mark 6 for about 20 minutes. Cut into fingers while warm and cool on a wire tray.

Orange cinnamon crisps

100 g (4 oz) butter
75 g (3 oz) caster sugar
1 egg yolk
grated rind of 1 orange
150 g (5 oz) self raising flour
5 ml (1 level tsp) ground cinnamon
50–75g (2–3 oz) chopped almonds

Makes 20–24

Cream together the butter and sugar until light and fluffy. Beat in the egg yolk and orange rind. Sift together the flour and cinnamon and stir them into the creamed mixture to give a smooth dough. Work it gently with your hands until smooth, then form it into a neat log shape. Cut 20–24 even slices; roll each into a ball and then roll the balls in the chopped almonds. Place them on greased baking sheets, well apart, and flatten slightly. Bake at 190°C (375°F) mark 5 for 15–20 minutes. Cool on a wire rack.

Herb scones with rosemary

50 g (2 oz) butter or margarine
225 g (8 oz) self raising flour
1·25 ml (¼ level tsp) salt
2·5 ml (½ level tsp) dried rosemary or
    7·5 ml (1½ tsps) fresh rosemary
about 150 ml (¼ pt) milk
beaten egg or milk to glaze

Makes about 10

In a bowl, rub the fat into the flour and salt until the mixture resembles fine breadcrumbs. Add the rosemary. Stir in enough milk to give a fairly soft but manageable dough. Turn it on to a floured board and knead very lightly. Roll the dough out to about 2 cm

($\frac{3}{4}$ in) thick or pat it out with your hand. Cut about 10 rounds with a 5-cm (2-in) cutter or cut into triangles with a sharp knife – re-knead as necessary. Place the scones on a baking sheet and brush the tops with egg or milk. Bake in the oven at 230°C (450°F) mark 8, for about 10 minutes. Cool them on a wire rack.

Cheese scones

75–100 g (3–4 oz) grated Cheddar cheese
1·25 ml ($\frac{1}{4}$ level tsp) celery salt

Make as for herb scones, using the above ingredients in place of the rosemary.

Spicy scones

50 g (2 oz) currants
30 ml (2 level tbsps) caster sugar
2·5 ($\frac{1}{2}$ level tsp) mixed spice

Make as for herb scones, using the above ingredients in place of the rosemary.

Fruit scones

30 ml (2 level tbsps) sultanas
45 ml (3 level tbsps) chopped walnuts
50 g (2 oz) soft brown sugar
2·5 ml ($\frac{1}{2}$ level tsp) ground cinnamon

Make as for herb scones, using the above ingredients in place of the rosemary.

Ginger meringues with almond cream

2 egg whites
45–60 ml (3–4 level tbsps) granulated sugar
5 ml (1 level tsp) ground ginger
45–60 ml (3–4 level tbsps) caster sugar
45 ml (3 level tbsps) chopped almonds
150 ml ($\frac{1}{4}$ pt) double cream
a few drops of almond essence

Makes 6–8 pairs

Line 2–3 baking sheets with oiled greaseproof paper or non-stick (silicone treated) paper. Whisk the egg whites until very stiff, add the granulated sugar and whisk again until the mixture regains its stiffness. Mix together the ground ginger and caster sugar and fold them into the egg whites very lightly, using a metal spoon. Fold in the chopped almonds. Place the mixture in spoonfuls on the baking sheets and dry off in the oven at 130°C (250°F) mark $\frac{1}{4}$ for several hours, until the meringues are dry and crisp but still white; they should come off the baking sheets easily. If they begin to brown, prop the oven door open a little. Allow them to cool on a wire rack.

To finish, whip the cream with the almond essence until it just holds its shape. Sandwich the meringues in pairs with the cream a short time before required.

Note The unfilled meringue shells keep well in an airtight container for a week or two.

Spice doughnuts

700 g (1$\frac{1}{2}$ lb) plain flour
20 ml (4 level tsps) baking powder
2·5 ml ($\frac{1}{2}$ level tsp) ground nutmeg
2·5 ml ($\frac{1}{2}$ level tsp) salt
3 eggs, beaten
200 g (7 oz) caster sugar
150 ml ($\frac{1}{4}$ pt) milk
50 g (2 oz) butter, melted and cooled
5 ml (1 tsp) vanilla essence
oil for deep frying
caster sugar for coating

Makes about 20

Sift the flour, baking powder, nutmeg

and salt. Beat the eggs and caster sugar with a wire whisk until thick and frothy. Gradually stir these into the flour mixtue along with the milk, butter and vanilla essence. Knead the mixture with your hands until the dough can be gathered into a smooth ball, then cover the bowl with a damp cloth and leave in the refrigerator for at least 30 minutes. Roll out the dough on a lightly floured surface to about 1 cm ($\frac{1}{2}$ in) thick. With a 6·5-cm ($2\frac{1}{2}$-in) biscuit cutter, stamp out as many doughnuts as possible without re-rolling, cutting a hole in the centre with a 2-cm ($\frac{3}{4}$-in) cutter. Do not re-roll the scraps or you will find the doughnuts may be tough; instead use the small cutter to stamp out smaller rounds from the scraps. Refrigerate until needed.

Pour the oil into a deep fat pan to a depth of about 7 cm ($2\frac{3}{4}$ in), and heat to 182°C (360°F). Deep fry the doughnuts 4 or 5 at a time. Drain on kitchen paper and toss in caster sugar.

Variations

1. Mix 5 ml (1 level tsp) ground nutmeg with 50 g (2 oz) caster sugar and use for coating instead of plain sugar, after frying.

2. Omit the nutmeg from the dough and mix 5 ml (1 level tsp) ground cinnamon with 50 g (2 oz) caster sugar to use for coating after frying.

3. Lemon and Honey Syrup for coating:
   225 g (8 oz) granulated sugar
   150 ml ($\frac{1}{4}$ pt) water
   15 ml (1 tbsp) lemon juice
   5 ml (1 level tsp) finely grated lemon rind
   75 g (3 oz) thin honey

Place the sugar, water and lemon juice in a saucepan, heat slowly to dissolve the sugar, then bring to the boil. Continue to boil until the syrup reaches 110°C (230°F) on a sugar-boiling thermometer. Reduce the heat to low, add the lemon rind and honey and simmer for 5 minutes. When the doughnuts are cooked, drain as usual and prick in three or four places with a fork. Dip them in the warm syrup and serve at once.

Gingerbread men

225 g (8 oz) golden syrup
175 g (6 oz) butter
550 g ($1\frac{1}{4}$ lb) self raising flour
5 ml (1 level tsp) salt
10 ml (2 level tsps) ground cinnamon
10 ml (2 level tsps) ground ginger
100 g (4 oz) demerara sugar
1 egg, beaten
currants or glacé icing, for decoration

Makes 20–24

Heat the syrup and butter gently in a saucepan until melted. Sift the flour, salt and spices together and mix with the demerara sugar. Make a well in the centre of the dry ingredients, pour in the syrup, butter and the egg and mix well, then knead lightly until smooth. If the mixture is too sticky to roll out, chill it for about 15 minutes until stiff enough to handle.

Roll out to about 0·5 cm ($\frac{1}{4}$ in) thick on a lightly floured board. Cut out the shapes with a gingerbread man cutter or use a sharp knife and a template cut out from cardboard. Place the men on lightly greased baking sheets and bake at 180°C (350°F) mark 4 for 12–15 minutes, until golden brown. Decorate whilst hot with currants for eyes, or when cold with glacé icing.

Swedish cardamom cake

125 g (4 oz) butter
225 g (8 oz) caster sugar
10 ml (2 level tsps) ground cardamom
1 large egg, beaten
150 ml (¼ pt) single cream
350 g (12 oz) self raising flour

For icing
75 g (3 oz) icing sugar, sifted
10 ml (2 tsps) lemon juice
grated lemon rind for decoration

Grease a 23-cm (9-in), 1·7-l (3-pt) ring mould and dust it with flour. Melt the butter and pour it over the sugar in a bowl. Beat in the cardamom, egg and cream, then fold in the sifted flour. Turn the mixture into the prepared tin and bake in the oven at 180°C (350°F) mark 4 for 40–45 minutes. Turn the cake out on to a wire rack to cool.

Blend the icing sugar to a smooth paste with the lemon juice and spoon on to the cake, letting it run down the sides. Decorate at once with finely grated lemon rind and leave to set.

Easter spice biscuits

75 g (3 oz) butter or margarine
50 g (2 oz) caster sugar
1 egg, separated
175 g (6 oz) self raising flour
pinch of salt
1·25 ml (¼ level tsp) ground nutmeg
1·25 ml (¼ level tsp) ground cinnamon
25 g (1 oz) currants
25 g (1 oz) chopped mixed peel
15–30 ml (1–2 tbsps) milk
a little caster sugar

Makes 15–20

Cream the butter and sugar and beat in the egg yolk. Sift the flour with the salt and spices and fold it into the creamed mixture with the currants and mixed peel. Add enough milk to give a fairly soft dough. Roll out the dough fairly thinly and cut into rounds, using a fluted 6·5-cm (2½-in) cutter. Put the biscuits on to lightly greased baking sheets. Bake in the oven at 200°C (400°F) mark 6 for about 15 minutes. After 10 minutes brush the biscuits with egg white, sprinkle with caster sugar and continue baking. Cool on a wire rack.

Sesame seed crescents

120 ml (8 level tbsps) toasted sesame
    seeds (see below)
100 g (3½ oz) butter
100 g (3½ oz) caster sugar
1 egg
200 g (7 oz) plain flour
10 ml (2 level tsps) baking powder
5 ml (1 level tsp) ground mace
pinch of salt
milk, if needed

Makes about 20

To toast the sesame seeds, spread them out in a large shallow baking tin (a Swiss roll tin). Toast in a pre-heated oven at 180°C (350°F) mark 4 for about 20 minutes or until lightly browned. Turn the seeds occasionally during toasting. Cream the butter and sugar together in a bowl and stir in the egg. Sift together the flour, baking powder, mace and salt. Add the flour to the creamed mixture and mix to a soft dough. Add a little milk if necessary. Roll dough into about 24 small sausage shapes, each 7·5 cm (3 in) long. Then roll them in the toasted sesame seeds. Place the rolls on ungreased baking sheets, curving the ends of each one round to form a crescent. Bake in the oven at 190°C (375°F) mark 5 for 15–20 minutes or until golden brown. Cool the crescents on a wire rack. Store in an airtight container.

Mandarin spice gâteau

175 g (6 oz) butter
175 g (6 oz) soft light brown sugar
3 large eggs
175 g (6 oz) self raising flour
5 ml (1 level tsp) mixed spice
100 g (4 oz) shelled walnuts, chopped
300 ml (½ pt) double cream
312-g (11-oz) can mandarin oranges, drained and juice reserved

For glaze
5 ml (1 level tsp) arrowroot
2·5 ml (½ level tsp) mixed spice

Grease and base-line two 20·5-cm (8-in) sandwich tins. Cream together the butter and sugar until light and fluffy then beat in the eggs. Sift the flour with the spice and fold it into the mixture with the walnuts. Divide the mixture between the tins and bake at 180°C (350°F) mark 4 for 30–35 minutes. Turn out the cakes and cool them on a wire rack.

Whip the cream until thick and fold the mandarins through. Use most of the cream to sandwich the two cake layers together. Measure 75 ml (5 tbsps) mandarin juice and blend a little with the arrowroot and mixed spice. Add the remaining measured juice and heat it gently, stirring until the mixture thickens and clears. Cook for a further minute, stirring, then brush whilst still hot over the top of the cake. Place the remaining cream and fruit in the centre of the top layer. Chill to set the cream before serving.

Drinks and Dressings

Classic mayonnaise

1 egg yolk
2·5 ml ($\frac{1}{2}$ level tsp) dry mustard
2·5 ml ($\frac{1}{2}$ level tsp) salt
1·25 ml ($\frac{1}{4}$ level tsp) pepper
2·5 ml ($\frac{1}{2}$ level tsp) sugar
about 150 ml ($\frac{1}{4}$ pt) oil
15 ml (1 tbsp) white distilled or wine
  vinegar

Makes about 300 ml ($\frac{1}{2}$ pt)

Put the egg yolk into a basin with the seasonings and sugar. Mix thoroughly, then add the oil drop by drop, stirring briskly with a wooden spoon the whole time or use a whisk, until the sauce is thick and smooth. If it becomes too thick, add a little of the vinegar. When all the oil has been added, stir in the vinegar and mix thoroughly. If you prefer, use lemon juice instead of the vinegar or half lemon juice and half vinegar. A hand held electric mixer or blender can also be used for making mayonnaise.

Variations

To 150 ml ($\frac{1}{4}$ pt) mayonnaise add:
1. 5 ml (1 level tsp) dried chives or 15 ml (1 tbsp) fresh chopped chives and 1·25 ml ($\frac{1}{4}$ level tsp) celery salt
2. 2·5 ml ($\frac{1}{2}$ level tsp) dried tarragon or 7·5 ml ($1\frac{1}{2}$ tsps) fresh chopped tarragon and 2·5 ml ($\frac{1}{2}$ level tsp) dried parsley or 7·5 ml ($1\frac{1}{2}$ tsps) fresh chopped parsley
3. 5 ml (1 level tsp) tomato paste, 1·25 ($\frac{1}{4}$ level tsp) paprika pepper and 5 ml (1 tsp) chopped olives

French salad dressing

1·25 ml ($\frac{1}{4}$ level tsp) salt
freshly ground black pepper
1·25 ml ($\frac{1}{4}$ level tsp) dry mustard
1·25 ml ($\frac{1}{4}$ level tsp) sugar
15 ml (1 tbsp) vinegar
30 ml (2 tbsps) salad oil

Put the salt, pepper, mustard and sugar into a bowl, or lidded container, add the vinegar and stir or shake until well blended. Whisk in the oil gradually or add to the container and shake. The oil does separate on standing so whisk or shake the dressing immediately before use.
Note The proportion of oil to vinegar varies according to individual taste; if you prefer, increase the oil to 45 ml (3 tbsps). Malt, wine, tarragon or any other vinegar may be used.

Variations

To the basic dressing add:
1. 1·25 ml ($\frac{1}{4}$ level tsp) minced garlic or 1 clove garlic, skinned and crushed
2. 2·5 ml ($\frac{1}{2}$ level tsp) dried chives or 7·5 ml ($1\frac{1}{2}$ tsps) fresh chopped chives
3. 2·5–5 ml ($\frac{1}{2}$–1 level tsp) curry powder
4. 2·5 ml ($\frac{1}{2}$ level tsp) dried parsley or 7·5 ml ($1\frac{1}{2}$ tsps) fresh chopped parsley, 2·5 ml ($\frac{1}{2}$ level tsp) dried marjoram or 7·5 ml ($1\frac{1}{2}$ tsps) fresh chopped marjoram and a pinch of dried thyme.
5. 2·5 ml ($\frac{1}{2}$ level tsp) dried mint or 7·5 ml ($1\frac{1}{2}$ tsps) fresh chopped mint
6. 1·25 ml ($\frac{1}{4}$ level tsp) caraway seeds and 2·5 ml ($\frac{1}{2}$ level tsp) dried thyme or 7·5 ml ($1\frac{1}{2}$ tsps) fresh chopped thyme

Rémoulade dressing

1 spring onion
$\frac{1}{4}$ green pepper
1·25 ml ($\frac{1}{4}$ level tsp) dried parsley or
   5 ml (1 tsp) fresh chopped parsley
1·25 ml ($\frac{1}{4}$ level tsp) dried chervil or
   5 ml (1 tsp) fresh chopped chervil
1·25 ml ($\frac{1}{4}$ level tsp) dried tarragon or
   5 ml (1 tsp) fresh chopped tarragon
300 ml ($\frac{1}{2}$ pt) mayonnaise
10 ml (2 tsps) Tabasco sauce
1·25 ml ($\frac{1}{4}$ level tsp) garlic salt
5 ml (1 tsp) lemon juice
pepper

Prepare the spring onion and chop it finely, including some of the green stem. Finely chop the green pepper. Mix these together in a bowl and add the remaining ingredients. Mix well and chill for 1–2 hours.

Dill cream dressing

150 ml (5 fl oz) soured cream
2·5 ml ($\frac{1}{2}$ level tsp) onion salt
10 ml (2 level tsps) dried parsley or
   30 ml (2 tbsps) chopped fresh parsley
5 ml (1 level tsp) dried dill weed or 15 ml
   (1 tbsp) chopped fresh dill
salt
pepper

Put all the ingredients into a bowl and mix well together. Allow to infuse for at least 15 minutes. Serve as a dressing for coleslaw or cucumber salads.

Sweet yoghurt dressing

150 ml (5 fl oz) natural yoghurt
10 ml (2 tsps) clear honey
5 ml (1 level tsp) dried mint or 15 ml
   (1 tbsp) chopped fresh mint or lemon
   balm

Put all the ingredients into a bowl and mix well together. Allow to infuse at least 15 minutes. Use as a dressing for fresh fruit such as strawberries or apples.

Parsley butter (maître d'hôtel)

100 g (4 oz) butter
10 ml (2 level tsps) dried parsley or
   30 ml (2 tbsps) finely chopped fresh
   parsley
good squeeze of lemon juice
salt
cayenne pepper

Cream the butter until soft. Add to it the remaining ingredients and beat together. Shape the butter into a roll and wrap it in greaseproof paper or kitchen foil. Leave in the refrigerator to harden. To serve, cut into pats about 0·5 cm ($\frac{1}{4}$ in) thick. Serve with grilled white fish, steak or egg dishes.

Tarragon butter

100 g (4 oz) butter
10 ml (2 level tsps) dried tarragon or
   30 ml (2 tbsps) chopped fresh tarragon
salt
freshly ground black pepper

Prepare as for parsley butter. Serve with grilled chicken or fish.

Mint butter

100 g (4 oz) butter
5 ml (1 level tsp) dried mint or 15 ml
   (1 tbsp) chopped fresh mint
salt
freshly ground black pepper

Prepare as for parsley butter. Serve with grilled lamb, carrots, peas, new potatoes.

Mixed herb butter

100 g (4 oz) butter
1·25 ml ($\frac{1}{4}$ level tsp) dried chervil or 5 ml
  (1 tsp) chopped fresh chervil
1·25 ml ($\frac{1}{4}$ level tsp) dried chives or 5 ml
  (1 tsp) chopped fresh chives
1·25 ml ($\frac{1}{4}$ level tsp) dried thyme or 5 ml
  (1 tsp) chopped fresh thyme
2·5 ml ($\frac{1}{2}$ level tsp) dried parsley or 7·5 ml
  (1$\frac{1}{2}$ tsps) chopped fresh parsley
5 ml (1 tsp) finely chopped onion

Prepare as for parsley butter. Serve with grills of all sorts.

Chive butter

100 g (4 oz) butter
5 ml (1 level tsp) dried chives or 15 ml
  (1 tbsp) chopped fresh chives
5 ml (1 tsp) lemon juice
salt
freshly ground black pepper

Prepare as for parsley butter. Serve with grilled gammon steaks, new potatoes and leeks.

Rosemary butter

100 g (4 oz) butter
2·5 ml ($\frac{1}{2}$ level tsp) dried rosemary or
  7·5 ml (1$\frac{1}{2}$ tsps) chopped fresh rosemary
salt
freshly ground black pepper

Prepare as for parsley butter. Serve with grilled lamb, noodles, and pasta dishes.

Cinnamon butter

Cream together 50 g (2 oz) butter, 50 g (2 oz) caster sugar and 10 ml (2 level tsps) ground cinnamon. Use as a filling for Danish pastries or spread on to hot toast or warm scones.

Piccalilli

1·4 kg (3 lb) marrow
450 g (1 lb) cauliflower florets
100 g (4 oz) green beans, sliced
225 g (8 oz) onions, skinned and sliced
$\frac{1}{2}$ large cucumber, peeled and diced
350 g (12 oz) salt
150 g (5 oz) sugar
1·1 l (2 pt) white distilled vinegar
40 g (1$\frac{1}{2}$ oz) dry mustard
45 ml (3 level tbsps) ground ginger
45 ml (3 level tbsps) flour
30 ml (2 level tbsps) turmeric

Makes about 3·2 kg (7 lb)

Peel the marrow, remove the seeds and dice the flesh. Layer all the vegetables with the salt in a large bowl; cover and leave to stand for 24 hours. Drain the vegetables. It is important to rinse off any undissolved salt. Put the sugar, 900 ml (1$\frac{1}{2}$ pt) of the vinegar and the vegetables in a large pan and bring to the boil. Simmer for 20 minutes. Blend together all the other ingredients with the remaining 300 ml ($\frac{1}{2}$ pt) vinegar. Stir this into the vegetables; bring to the boil and cook for 3 minutes. Pot and cover with vinegar proof tops.

Indian chutney

450 g (1 lb) cooking apples, peeled,
  cored and sliced
225 g (8 oz) onions, skinned and coarsely
  chopped
4 cloves garlic, skinned and crushed
25 g (1 oz) salt
450 g (1 lb) soft brown sugar
1·1 l (2 pt) malt vinegar
225 g (8 oz) stoned raisins, chopped
25 g (1 oz) ground ginger
15 ml (1 level tbsp) cayenne pepper
25 g (1 oz) dry mustard

Makes about 1·1 kg (2$\frac{1}{2}$ lb)

Simmer the apples, onions, garlic, salt, sugar and vinegar uncovered until quite soft and reduced. Put through a fine sieve. Add the raisins, ginger, cayenne and mustard, mix well and leave in a warm but not hot place until the following day, to thicken. Pot and seal with vinegar proof tops.

This curry accompaniment has the consistency of thick sauce.

Spiced apples

30 ml (2 level tbsps) whole cloves
1 stick cinnamon
5 ml (1 level tsp) ground allspice
600 ml (1 pt) white vinegar
900 g (2 lb) sugar
2·5 ml ($\frac{1}{2}$ level tsp) salt
900 g (2 lb) cooking apples, peeled, cored
  and quartered

Put all the ingredients except the apples into a saucepan. Heat gently to dissolve the sugar, then bring to the boil. Add the apples and cook them gently until soft but not mushy. Drain the apple segments and pack them in warm jars. Boil the syrup until it is beginning to thicken. Strain it and pour it over the apples. Seal the jars with vinegar proof tops. Serve with pork or ham.

Spiced prunes

900 g (2 lb) prunes
450 g (1 lb) sugar
400 ml ($\frac{3}{4}$ pt) vinegar
thinly pared rind of $\frac{1}{4}$ lemon
2 whole cloves
5 ml (1 level tsp) ground allspice
small piece root ginger
1 cinnamon stick

Makes about 900 g (2 lb)

Prick the prune skins with a pin, then soak them in water overnight. Next day, dissolve the sugar in the vinegar and add the lemon rind and spices. Add the drained prunes and boil gently for about 15 minutes. Drain the prunes and pack them into hot jars. Reduce the vinegar by fast boiling until syrupy, and strain it over the prunes. Cover with vinegar proof tops. Serve with roast pork or turkey.

Spicy apricot stuffing

75 g (3 oz) dried apricots
75 g (3 oz) fresh white breadcrumbs
1·25 ml ($\frac{1}{4}$ level tsp) mixed spice
5 ml (1 level tsp) dried parsley or 15 ml
  (1 tbsp) chopped fresh parsley
1·25 ml ($\frac{1}{4}$ level tsp) salt
1·25 ml ($\frac{1}{4}$ level tsp) pepper
15 ml (1 tbsp) lemon juice
25 g (1 oz) butter, melted
1 small egg, beaten

Soak the apricots overnight in cold water. Drain off the liquid and chop the fruit. Stir in the breadcrumbs, spice, parsley, salt, pepper, lemon juice and butter. Bind with the egg and use as a stuffing for pork, lamb or chicken.

Sage and onion stuffing

2 large onions, skinned and chopped
knob of butter
125 g (4 oz) fresh white breadcrumbs
10 ml (2 level tsps) dried sage or 30 ml
  (2 tbsps) chopped fresh sage
salt and pepper

Put the onions in a pan of cold water, bring to the boil and cook until tender – about 10 minutes. Drain them well, add the other ingredients and mix well. Use for stuffing pork or chicken.

Herb stuffing

25–50 g (1–2 oz) cooked ham or bacon
25 g (1 oz) shredded suet
125 g (4 oz) fresh white breadcrumbs
5 ml (1 level tsp) dried parsley or 15 ml
  (1 tbsp) chopped fresh parsley
10 ml (2 level tsps) dried mixed herbs
grated rind of ½ lemon
salt and pepper
beaten egg to mix
milk or stock to bind

Finely chop the ham or bacon then mix with the suet and breadcrumbs. Add the parsley, mixed herbs and lemon rind. Season well and add the beaten egg with milk or stock, if required, to bind. Use as a stuffing for veal, shoulder of lamb, liver or chicken.

Herb bread

100 g (4 oz) butter
2·5 ml garlic granules or 2 cloves garlic,
  skinned and crushed
1·25 ml (¼ level tsp) dried parsley or 5 ml
  (1 tsp) chopped fresh parsley
squeeze of lemon juice
1 French loaf

Beat the butter until soft. Soak the garlic granules in a little warm water to soften, then drain and mix the garlic, parsley and lemon juice into the butter. Cut the loaf diagonally from the top almost to the bottom at 5-cm (2-in) intervals. Spread the butter on one side of each slice and wrap the loaf tightly in kitchen foil. Heat in the oven at 180°C (350°F) mark 4 for about 15 minutes, until the butter has melted and the bread is crisp. Serve hot.

Variations

Replace the garlic with,

1. 5 ml (1 level tsp) dried thyme or
   15 ml (1 tbsp) chopped fresh thyme
2. 5 ml (1 level tsp) dried sage or 15 ml
   (1 tbsp) chopped fresh sage

To either of these herbs, add onion salt to taste and prepare as for garlic bread.

Herb croûtons

4 thick slices bread, about 125 g (4–5 oz
  total weight)
45 ml (3 tbsps) cooking oil
1·25 ml (¼ level tsp) onion salt
1·25 ml (¼ level tsp) garlic salt
1·25 ml (¼ level tsp) dried sage or 5 ml
  (1 tsp) chopped fresh sage
10 ml (2 level tsps) dried parsley or 30 ml
  (2 tbsps) chopped fresh parsley
pepper

Cut the bread into dice. Place them on a baking sheet and put in the oven at 200°C (400°F) mark 6, for about 10 minutes or until the bread is golden brown. Remove from the oven. Put the oil into a saucepan. Add the salts, herbs and pepper. Heat until warm, then add the bread cubes and mix thoroughly together. Serve with soups, or on salad or vegetable dishes.

Cheese dip

225 g (8 oz) cream cheese
30–45 ml (2–3 tbsps) single cream
2 spring onions, finely chopped
2·5 ml (½ level tsp) dried *fines herbes*

Blend all the ingredients to a soft cream. Serve in a small dish, with savoury biscuits, carrot sticks and other dunks.

Variations

To the cheese and cream only add

1. Garlic salt and freshly ground black pepper to taste
2. 15 ml (1 level tbsp) dried chives or 45 ml (3 tbsps) chopped fresh chives. The dried chives should be reconstituted in hot water before use.

Virginia mint julep

9 leaves of fresh mint
5 ml (1 level tsp) sugar or sugar syrup
crushed ice
a good measure of Bourbon whisky

Serves 1

Put 6 leaves of mint into a cold glass. Add the sugar and crush the two together. Fill the glass with crushed ice and pour in the whisky, stirring well.

Spicy fruit punch

600 ml (1 pt) fresh or canned orange juice
300 ml ($\frac{1}{2}$ pt) canned pineapple juice
juice and thinly pared rind of 1 lemon
2·5 ml ($\frac{1}{2}$ level tsp) ground nutmeg
6 cloves
2·5 ml ($\frac{1}{2}$ level tsp) ground mixed spice
600 ml (1 pt) water
100–175 g (4–6 oz) sugar
6 splits of ginger ale, chilled
crushed ice
twists of lemon or orange peel for garnish

Makes about 20 glasses

Mix the fruit juices, lemon rind and spices in a large jug. Put the water and sugar into a saucepan and heat gently to dissolve the sugar. Cool and add the syrup to the other ingredients in the jug. Chill. Strain the liquid and add the ginger ale and some crushed ice before serving. Garnish with the peel.

Glühwein

6 lumps of sugar
2 slices of lemon
2 slices of orange
2 cloves
1 bottle red wine
1 cinnamon stick

Makes about 750 ml ($1\frac{1}{4}$ pt)

Put all the ingredients into a saucepan and slowly bring almost to the boil. Remove from the heat, strain and serve at once.

Spiced cider punch

1·1 l (2 pt) cider
7·5–15 ml ($\frac{1}{2}$–1 level tbsp) sugar
juice of 1 orange
juice of $\frac{1}{2}$ lemon
pinch of ground ginger
pinch of ground nutmeg
1 cinnamon stick
1 orange stuck with 8 cloves, then sliced

Makes about 1·3 l ($2\frac{1}{4}$ pt)

Put all the ingredients into a saucepan and bring to serving temperature but do not boil. Serve hot.

Index